Bet͟ ͟

and Boonville

by Matt Williams

A SAMUEL FRENCH ACTING EDITION

SAMUEL
FRENCH
FOUNDED 1830

New York Hollywood London Toronto

SAMUELFRENCH.COM

BETWEEN DAYLIGHT AND BOONVILLE was first presented by the Cherubs Guild Corporation, Carol Avila, Lesley Starbuck, and Hillary Wyler at the Wonderhorse Theatre in New York City on September 11, 1980. It was directed by John David Lutz; the scenery and costumes were by James Stewart; and the lighting was by Jo Mayer. The cast, in order of appearance, was as follows:

STACY .... Wendy Ann Finnegan
CARLA .... Rebecca Guy
JIMMY .... Christian Slater
BOBBY .... Sean Mullane
CYRIL .... Kevin McClarnon
MARLENE .... Lorna Johnson
LORETTE .... Georgia Southcotte
WANDA .... Laurie Ross

BETWEEN DAYLIGHT AND BOONVILLE was subsequently presented by the University of Evansville, Evansville, Indiana, on November 13, 1981. It was directed by John David Lutz and the scenery, costumes and lighting were by S. Judson Mclean. The cast, in order of appearance was as follows:

STACY .... Danica Vasilchek
CARLA .... Dede Lovejoy
JIMMY .... Bryan Horstman
BOBBY .... Bradley Horstman
CYRIL .... Dennis Ward
MARLENE......................... Christia Stinson
LORETTE......................... Patricia Carroll
WANDA............................... Julie Fishell

This production, as a part of the American College Theatre Festival, was presented in the Terrace Theatre of the John F. Kennedy Center for the Performing Arts on April 19–20, 1982.

3

CAST OF CHARACTERS

STACY — 8, Carla's daughter

CARLA* — mid-20's, mother to Stacy

CYRIL — early 30's, Carla's friend, a coal miner

MARLENE — mid-30's, Carla's best friend, six and a half or seven months pregnant

JIMMIE — 10, Marlene's son

BOBBY — 7, Marlene's son

WANDA — late 20's, Cyril's good friend, a widow

LORETTE — early 60's, friend to Marlene and Carla

---

*A note about casting the role of CARLA:

The character should be child-like but never childish. It is important the actress playing CARLA possess a warmth and naivete.

Between Daylight and Boonville

SETTING: *The setting is a temporary trailor court in the strip mining country of southern Indiana. There are two trailers (or portions of them) on stage. The s.l. trailer, CARLA'S trailer, has a porch and steps attached to it. The trailer is old but generally well kept. Next to the trailer's porch is a water faucet, mop and bucket. The trailer s.r. is in need of repairs and new paint. This is MARLENE'S trailer. Instead of a porch, concrete blocks have been stacked to make steps. In the clearing between the trailers is a make-shift recreational area. There is a metal lawn set consisting of three chairs and a round table. The lawn furniture was white at one time but is now a dull gray because of the perpetual coal dust. There is junk scattered about the area such as old tires, car parts and a few broken toys. There is a gas tank on stilts near the rear of MARLENE'S trailer, which serves as a "horse" for the kids or home base when they play Hide-N-Seek. DS.R. sits an old tractor tire filled with sand and dirt, which serves as a sand box for the children. There are no trees and no grass, only a few weeds grow around the edges of the trailers.*

TIME: *A hot day in August.*

The lights come up and we discover STACY sitting in the sand box talking to her doll and a stuffed

7

animal. STACY is a skinny eight year old girl with long, sand colored hair. She wears cut off shorts, a tattered T-shirt and is barefooted. From the trailer s.l., *we hear a radio playing country and western music.*

STACY. (*to the doll*) Margaret is the mother. There's five of them. Three boys and two girls.
CARLA. (*inside the trailer*) Stacy.
STACY. There was six, but one of them died.
CARLA. Staaaaaaaceeeee!
STACY. What?
CARLA. Where are you?
STACY. Here.
CARLA. Where?
STACY. Here!

(*CARLA sticks her head out the trailer's window. CARLA is twenty-six years old, has reddish-brown hair and a small, compact body. She would be described as cute, with an almost child-like face. She is energetic and quick. CARLA wears faded jeans and a work shirt with the tails tied about her midriff.*)

CARLA. What'd I tell you to do? Why ain't you packed? You're suppose to be packin'.
STACY. I'm busy.
CARLA. Stacy, get in here and pack. And I mean right now. I ain't foolin' with you girl.
STACY. I don't wanna pack.
CARLA. Get goin'.
STACY. Wait till Dad gets home.

CARLA. Quit that whinin' and get packed. We're leavin'. (*CARLA ducks back into the trailer. STACY picks up her doll and stuffed animal.*)

STACY. Come on. I gotta go pack. Come on. (*CARLA comes out of the trailer carrying two large suitcases. She has trouble maneuvering on the small porch and gets one of the suitcases caught in the railing.*)

CARLA. Get movin' girl. Stacy I swear. If you had to haul ass, you'd have to make two trips. And get some shoes on. I don't want you cuttin' your feet on another pop top.

STACY. Ohhh, do I have to?

CARLA. Go!

STACY. Do I have to wear my shoes?

CARLA. Yes, you do.

STACY. They pinch. They hurt my feet.

CARLA. Somethin' else be hurtin' a lot more if you don't get a move on. And turn off that radio in there. Noise drivin' me crazy.

STACY. Momma, I don't want to wear my shoes!

(*As CARLA struggles with the suitcases, there is a distant blast of dynamite that causes her to drop one of the suitcases. Clothing scatters everywhere. The dynamite also causes the dogs in the kennel behind the trailer to start barking and howling.*)

CARLA. Damnit to hell. Get in that trailer and get packed. No more back talk or I'm goin' to blister your butt! (*STACY runs inside. CARLA crosses back towards the dogs.*) Shut up! Quit that. Shut up now. Be quiet. (*The dogs gradually quiet down. CARLA begins picking up the scattered clothing.*) Staaacee. Only pack the clothes that fit you. Don't go packin' everything this time. We're travelin' light. And hurry so we can get out of here. And be careful in the kitchen.

STACY. (*from inside*) Where are we goin'?

CARLA. You let me worry about that. Get packed.

STACY. Okayee!

CARLA. You need me to help?

STACY. No.

CARLA. (*to herself*) Course you don't need help. I forget. You're a full grown eight year old woman. Don't need my help anymore.

(*JIMMIE bursts out of the trailer* s.r. *He is ten or eleven years old, wears cut off shorts, no shirt and is barefooted. He carries an old, leather horse's bridle.*)

JIMMIE. Hey, Carla.

CARLA. Hhmmmh.

JIMMIE. Where's Stacy?

CARLA. Inside.

JIMMIE. Can she come out?

CARLA. No, she can't.

JIMMIE. What are you doin'?

BOBBY. (*from inside MARLENE'S trailer*) Jimmie!

JIMMIE. Yes!

BOBBY. Jimmie, you got the bridle?

JIMMIE. Yes!

(*BOBBY comes out of the trailer. He is a small, shaggy haired boy of seven. He is dressed exactly like his older brother, JIMMIE.*)

BOBBY. Hey, Carla.

CARLA. Hi, Bobby.

BOBBY. Where's your daddy?

CARLA. What?

JIMMIE. He means your husband.

BOBBY. We're goin' to the woods. Can Larry come with us?

CARLA. He's at work.

BOBBY. Can Stacy come?

CARLA. No. She's busy right now.

JIMMIE. Doin' what?

BOBBY. Can she help us catch the pony?

CARLA. Look. Stacy's got things to do. You boys run along and quit botherin' me or I'll tell your mother. Ok?

BOBBY/JIMMIE. Ok.

BOBBY. Let me carry the bridle.

JIMMIE. I got it.

BOBBY. I want to.

JIMMIE. Here. Both of us can. We'll share.

BOBBY. Bye, Carla.

CARLA. Bye.

JIMMIE. Bye, Carla.

CARLA. Bye. (*JIMMIE and BOBBY exit.*) Stacy? (*There is no answer from inside.*) STAACEE!

STACY. (*inside*) What?

CARLA. You 'bout packed?

STACY. (*coming to the doorway*) Yes, but I can't find my shoes.

CARLA. Yes, you can.

STACY. I can't.

CARLA. Look for them.

STACY. I did.

CARLA. Look harder.

STACY. Can Margaret come with us?

CARLA. No!

STACY. Ohhh . . .

CARLA. Margaret is stayin' here. Forget Margaret and

find your shoes. (*STACY goes back inside the trailer. To herself.*) I swear that kid couldn't find her ass with both hands. Helpless. Totally helpless. Got to do everything around here. Everything . . .

(*While CARLA picks up the clothing and mumbles to herself, CYRIL enters. CYRIL is a short, stocky man in his mid-thirties with curly hair and a bounce to his walk. CYRIL wears work boots, jeans, an old baseball cap and a white T-shirt that accentuates his strong arms. CYRIL loves to talk, or more specifically, loves to hear himself talk. His left hand is bandaged. CYRIL spots CARLA bending over the suitcase. He tip toes up behind her and grabs her.*)

CYRIL. WAAAH!
CARLA. AAAHH!
CYRIL. Gotcha!
CARLA. (*chasing CYRIL*) Cyril, you son of a . . .
CYRIL. Ooooohhhh!
CARLA. I kill you . . .
CYRIL. Ah, come on.
CARLA. . . . you ever do that again.
CYRIL. Hey, now.
CARLA. I mean it.
CYRIL. Want to brighten your mornin'. (*CARLA gives up trying to catch him, so she begins throwing things.*)
CARLA. You dumb shit!
CYRIL. Yes I am. I most certainly am.
CARLA. (*throwing at him*) Ignorant.
CYRIL. Hey! Be careful.
CARLA. Scare me to death. I could've had a heart attack.

CYRIL. No you couldn't. You ain't got a heart.

CARLA. Stay away . . .

CYRIL. Besides you love it and you know it.

CARLA. I don't love nothin'.

CYRIL. Not even me?

CARLA. Especially you.

CYRIL. (*moving toward her*) You know you do. A little tweek on the cheek . . .

CARLA. Be quiet.

CYRIL. . . . make you meek, Carla Mae. (*CYRIL pinches her. CARLA chases him again.*)

CARLA. You think meek if I get my hands on you.

CYRIL. I wish you would get your hands on me. Real tight. Late at night. Make me feel allll right! (*beat*)

CARLA. Cyril, you ever hear yourself? You wouldn't say another word if you knew how ignorant you sounded. You act like an idiot most of the time.

CYRIL. But I'm happy.

CARLA. Ignorant! That's all you are. Ain't got a brain in your head. (*CARLA goes back to the clothes on the ground.*)

CYRIL. I may not be too bright, but at least I don't throw my clothes in the dirt.

CARLA. You're standin' on my blouse.

CYRIL. What you doin' with that suitcase? Goin' somewhere?

CARLA. You might say that.

CYRIL. I might say a lot of things. Like, "Carla Mae, where are you goin'?"

CARLA. Nowhere.

CYRIL. Does Larry know you're goin' nowhere?

CARLA. You just love to bother me don't you?

CYRIL. No. I just love you. (*CYRIL grabs her hand and kisses it.*)

CARLA. (*pulling her hand away*) You silly . . .

CYRIL. I do.

CARLA. Why ain't you at work? You're supposed to be at the pits.

CYRIL. Ohhh, I can't. It's my sick hand, Carla Mae. See. Can't work.

CARLA. I saw you wavin' it around. What'd you do?

CYRIL. Drove a drill shaft right through that sucker yeaterday. It slipped and BAM! Right through. Didn't even feel it till Freddie Johnson pulled my hand free. Blood! Whew! Talk about blood. I looked down and my knees buckled and I could feel myself turnin' white. And I thought, "Oh, Lord. Here comes breakfast." There was blood everywhere. I couldn't believe it. Squirtin'. Sprayin'. Everywhere . . .

CARLA. Ok. Ok . . .

CYRIL. I swear I could put my hand up to my face and look right through it. Like a Life Saver. Hole in the middle.

CARLA. How long you goin' to be off?

CYRIL. Week. Ten days.

CARLA. A week, huh?

CYRIL. Or ten days. I don't like workin' those pits when they're dynamitin'. High wall is over a hundred and twenty feet tall at my end. Don't like to be around that dirt when they're messin' with that dynamite. Brings out the Kentucky Fried in me. Cluck, cluck . . . (*CYRIL does a bad imitation of a chicken.*)

CARLA. Does it hurt?

CYRIL. What?

CARLA. Your hand?

CYRIL. Course it hurts. But I'm a man. I can take it. I may be short, but I'm brave. Of course the pills the doctor gave me help a little. Only really hurts me when I get excited. Then it throbs. It throbs a lot when I'm around you, Carla Mae. Thump-Thump . . .

CARLA. Get away from me.

CYRIL. Thump-Thump . . .

CARLA. Larry didn't say nothin' about your hand.

CYRIL. He was workin' the other end of the pit when I did it. I was down with Big Jim when it happened.

CARLA. He's had a lot on his mind lately. Been worried about Margaret. How is she anyway?

CARLA. She's fine.

CYRIL. She's doin' ok?

CARLA. You can see for yourself. Right inside the trailer. In the kitchen. (*CYRIL goes to the trailer and looks inside.*)

CYRIL. The kitchen?

CARLA. Yes.

CYRIL. Good ol' Margaret.

CARLA. (*to herself*) Yeah, good ol' Margaret.

CYRIL. She's been around a long time. (*CYRIL goes inside.*) Whew! Damn! (*CYRIL comes out on the porch.*) What a mess! Gag a maggot in there.

CARLA. Listen, Cyril. Cyril, listen to me. (*CARLA grabs his arm.*)

CYRIL. Thump-Thump. Thump . . .

CARLA. Cyril, quit actin' so silly and listen to me. Can you do me a favor?

CYRIL. I can do anything.

CARLA. Can you give me a ride? In your truck?

CYRIL. Where?

CARLA. I don't know. Petersburg. Boonville. Just away. Somewhere Stacy and me can catch a bus.

CYRIL. I don't know.

CARLA. Could you? Please? Everyone else is at the pits and I don't have no way to get there.

CYRIL. When?

CARLA. Right now.

CYRIL. Now?

CARLA. Well, in a minute. Let me finish packin' and get Stacy and you drive us to a bus station.

CYRIL. I don't know if I can do that.

CARLA. Why?

CYRIL. Well, Larry . . .

CARLA. Forget Larry. Would you do it for me? Give me and Stacy a ride. Ok? Please?

CYRIL. Ok.

CARLA. You will?

CYRIL. Yes.

CARLA. Oh, Cyril . . .

CYRIL. But not right now.

CARLA. Why?

CYRIL. I got things to do.

CARLA. What?

CYRIL. Things.

CARLA. What?

CYRIL. I was on my way over to Wanda's . . .

CARLA. Wanda's!

CYRIL. . . . to pick up some things.

CARLA. Only thing you're goin' to pick up at Wanda's is the clap.

CYRIL. Carla Mae!

CARLA. It's true and you know it.

CYRIL. I ought to wash your mouth out with soap. You talk so nasty.

(*JIMMIE dashes up, dives to the ground and crawls under the trailer.*)

CYRIL. Hey, hot shot!

JIMMIE. Hey, Cyril.

CYRIL. Where you goin' in such a hurry?

JIMMIE. Under here.

CYRIL. I can see that. What for?

JIMMIE. Get a rope.

CYRIL. Need some help?

JIMMIE. Nope.

CARLA. Why you goin' over there?

CYRIL. I told you to pick up some things.

CARLA. What?

CYRIL. Cigarettes. I'm out and I don't feel like drivin' all the way to Skelly's with my hurt hand.

CARLA. Uh huh. Sure.

CYRIL. Really. I'm out of cigarettes.

CARLA. Don't lie to me.

(*JIMMIE crawls out from under the trailer with an old piece of rope.*)

CARLA. (*to CYRIL*) I ain't stupid.

CYRIL. What you need a rope for?

JIMMIE. We're gonna make a trap.

CYRIL. You still tryin' to catch that wild pony?

JIMMIE. Yep.

CYRIL. You guys never give up do you?

JIMMIE. Nope. (*JIMMIE exits.*)

CYRIL. (*calling after him*) What are you goin' to do when you catch him?

CARLA. Cigarettes ain't the only thing she's sellin' over in that trailer . . .

CYRIL. No. She's got milk and bread . . .

CARLA. And it sure as hell ain't the only thing you're buyin'.

CYRIL. That's not true. I never had to pay for it a day in my life. Women fight to give it away to me. I may be short, but I'm sexy.

CARLA. You'd jump on anything that walks. Even that scum whore Wanda.

CYRIL. I don't chase whores. They chase after me.

Anything that walks, talks or crawls. Tooth to toothless. Six to sixty. I love 'em all. Especially you, Carla Mae. Thump-Thump . . .

CARLA. You better get goin', Cyril. I don't want you to keep Wanda waitin' any longer than you have to.

CYRIL. Listen, I'll be glad to give you a ride . . .

CARLA. Get out of here.

CYRIL. I'll drive you anywhere you want to go. But not now. After 'while. Ok?

CARLA. Go get your cigarettes and quit botherin' me.

CYRIL. You know I'd do anything for you. I'd drive you to hell if that's where you wanted to go.

CARLA. You don't have to do that. I'm already there. (*CARLA turns away from CYRIL. He stares at her for a moment, then starts to go. CYRIL spots a pair of CARLA'S panties on the ground, picks them up and slips them on over his jeans.*)

CYRIL. Hey, Carla. (*CARLA does not answer, so CYRIL climbs up on one of the chairs.*) Carla Mae?

CARLA. What?

CYRIL. I told you I'd get in your pants. (*CARLA is caught between laughing and crying. She laughs at CYRIL, then gets angry at herself for laughing. The following exchange overlaps.*)

CARLA. You crazy . . . Get those off.

CYRIL. I'm goin' to keep them. Forever.

CARLA. Give 'em here. (*CARLA chases CYRIL.*)

CYRIL. Sleep with 'em.

CARLA. Give 'em to me.

CYRIL. . . . under my pillow.

CARLA. Right now.

CYRIL. I'm never goin' to wash 'em! (*CARLA catches CYRIL, jumps on his back and wrestles him to the ground. He protects his hurt hand.*)

CYRIL. Watch out for my hand!

CARLA. You goin' to give those back?

CYRIL. Hey! No fair ticklin'.

CARLA. How you like that!

CYRIL. Don't. No fair. Time out.

CARLA. You give up?

CYRIL. Don't tickle . . .

CARLA. You give?

CYRIL. Please don't tickle. I'm goin' to pee my pants

. . .

(*During the chase, MARLENE opens her trailer door and watches CYRIL and CARLA. MARLENE is a large boned woman about thirty-five years old, although she looks somewhat older. There is a tranquil quality about her, an aura of calm. She wears a faded sundress and thongs. She is six and a half to seven months pregnant.*)

CYRIL. Help me, Marlene. She's gonna kill me.

CARLA. Damn right I am.

MARLENE. You two at it again. You're worse than a couple of kids. (*CYRIL manages to throw off CARLA and run to MARLENE. He grabs a magazine from the stack she is holding and uses it as a sword.*)

CYRIL. Protect me momma. She's crazy.

MARLENE. Cyril, what are you . . .

CYRIL. She's nuts!

MARLENE. Be careful with my magazine.

CYRIL. (*to CARLA*) On guard! Touche!

CARLA. I'll touche your ass you little creep. (*CYRIL tosses the magazine back to MARLENE and runs offstage.*) You better run. Creep! (*CARLA, smiling broadly, tries to catch her breath. She notices*

MARLENE watching her and instantly wipes the smile from her face.)

MARLENE. What are you two at it about this time? What's he got on?

CARLA. Underwear.

MARLENE. What's he doin' with them on?

CARLA. They're mine

MARLENE. Yours?

CARLA. He stole 'em.

MARLENE. What are they . . . What are you up to? (*CARLA does not answer.*) Carla, what are you doin'?

(*LORETTE enters from behind CARLA'S trailer. LORETTE is in her early sixties, and wrinkled. She wears an ill fitting house coat, slippers and a pair of glasses that hang from a string around her neck. As always, she is smoking a Camel cigarette.*)

LORETTE. What in the hell is goin' on?

MARLENE. Hi, Lorette.

LORETTE. What's wrong over here?

MARLENE. Oh, Carla and Cyril are fightin' again.

LORETTE. Is that all? Hell, I thought one of the dogs got loose. (*LORETTE crosses to CARLA.*) You interrupted my mornin' movie with your yellin' and carryin' on . . . TO CATCH A THIEF with Cary Grant . . . (*LORETTE spots the suitcases.*) What are you doin'?

CARLA. I'm leavin'.

LORETTE. Ah, crap.

MARLENE. Oh, Lord.

CARLA. I really am, Marlene. I'm packed and I'm leavin' for good.

LORETTE. Carla, this is the third time this month. Not

even the end of August. Hell girl, you're packed more than you're unpacked.

CARLA. This time I'm dead serious. I'm leavin' this place for good. I ain't takin' no more.

MARLENE. (*repeating with CARLA*) " . . . I'm leavin' this place for good. I ain't takin' no more." I know all that. Now calm down.

CARLA. I am calm.

LORETTE. You mean I left Cary Grant over there in my trailer for this?

CARLA. I really am leavin'.

LORETTE. Yeah, and I'm Janet Gaynor.

CARLA. I am Lorette!

LORETTE. Don't get froggy with me and start jumpin' around. Why you leavin' now?

MARLENE. Is it Larry? What'd he do? Buy another truck?

LORETTE. You bored?

MARLENE. A dog? (*CARLA ignores them.*) Alright then. Come on, Lorette. She's in one of her moods. Leave her alone.

CARLA. I don't want to talk about it.

MARLENE. Alright with me.

CARLA. I just want to get out of here.

MARLENE. Ok. (*STACY comes out of the trailer.*)

STACY. I'm all packed, but I can't find my shoes.

CARLA. I told you to look!

STACY. I did.

CARLA. Did not.

STACY. Did too!

CARLA. Did not!

LORETTE. (*yelling*) Quit yellin'! Damn! Give me a headache. Carla, you have a nice trip. I'm goin' back home to Cary. (*LORETTE exits.*)

MARLENE. Hi, Stacy.

STACY. Hi.

MARLENE. How are you, honey?

STACY. Can't find my shoes.

MARLENE. You need me to help you?

STACY. No. I can find them. Mama, can we take a puppy?

CARLA. No. Leave the pups alone. Go find you shoes and bring your stuff out here. (*STACY goes back inside the trailer.*)

MARLENE. Why do you yell at that baby so much?

CARLA. I got to get her to listen don't I?

MARLENE. There's other ways. You're way too hard on her.

CARLA. Look at these clothes. They're filthy. (*CARLA separates the dirty clothes from the clean. MARLENE watches her for a moment.*)

MARLENE. Margaret had her pups, huh?

CARLA. Just take a peek inside the trailer. In the kitchen. Go ahead and look.

MARLENE. What's she doin' in the kitchen? (*MARLENE crosses and goes inside the trailer.*)

CARLA. Larry brought her in last night. I got dried blood and afterbirth all over my linoleum floor. Spent all day yesterday cleanin' that trailer. Spic-N-Spanned that floor on my hands and knees and he brings that coon dog in last night to have her puppies. Right in the middle of my kitchen floor.

MARLENE. (*coming out of the trailer*) Why couldn't she of had them in the kennel with the rest of them?

CARLA. Not Margaret! You don't let a prize coon dog just squat down and have her puppies anywhere. No, sir. She's got to be inside where there's shade, away from the heat and the flies and the other dogs. That's twelve hundred dollars worth of dog in there. God forbid she should have a fly land on her poody.

MARLENE. She is Larry's pride and joy. He's had her a long time. And it's not that big a mess. Really. Only a little blood. I'll help you clean it up. Spic-N-Span get that blood right up.

CARLA. I'm not touchin' that mess, Marlene. I mean it.

MARLENE. Well, it's too hot to fuss. Just sit down and relax and we'll clean it up later.

CARLA. I'm not touchin' it.

MARLENE. Don't think about it. Come on, sit down for a while before you have a heat stroke. It won't kill you to sit down for a minute.

CARLA. Well . . .

MARLENE. Whew! Can't believe it's this hot and not even noon.

CARLA. Cyril walked all over my clothes. Have to wash these out. (*CARLA goes inside the trailer for a wash tub, then crosses to the faucet and rinses out some of the clothing and hangs them on a clothes line* US. *as she and MARLENE talk.*)

MARLENE. Carla, that mess in there ain't no reason to get upset and leave. Don't think about it. You've started to leave before for a lot worse things than that. It's only a little blood.

CARLA. Oh, it ain't just the blood.

MARLENE. What is it then?

CARLA. Larry yelled at me.

MARLENE. So?

CARLA. He cussed me out and we had a big fight. I started to leave last night. But I knew he'd twist my head off if I walked out the door. He was so mad.

MARLENE. What about?

CARLA. One of the puppies. You see, I wasn't goin' to say nothin' about Margaret havin' her pups in the trailer. The whole time I kept thinkin'. I'm goin' to do like you do and not think about it. Forget the fact I scrubbed that linoleum floor all day on my hands and knees.

MARLENE. What happened?

CARLA. Margaret was lickin' one of the pups clean and she got excited tryin' to chew off the cord and she yanked all its guts out. Larry says it was my fault cause I made her nervous. I was watchin' TV and poppin' popcorn like nothin' was goin' on. Tryin' to be casual. Margaret got excited when I was in the kitchen and yanked too hard. So Larry starts yellin', holdin' up the dead puppy, wavin' it in front of my face. "You know how much you cost me? That's a thousand dollars worth of registered puppy guts on that floor. You dumb shit!"

MARLENE. Was he drunk?

CARLA. No. He didn't start drinkin' till after she had all her pups and I went to bed. Woke up this mornin' and there were empty beer cans all over the trailer.

MARLENE. He didn't hit you did he?

CARLA. He knows better than to try and hit me since I put that cigarette out on his chest.

MARLENE. Well, he didn't mean nothin' by it. Larry's just been real worried about Margaret that's all. Didn't mean nothin'. Big Jim does the same thing all the time. He yelled at you cause he didn't have nobody else to yell at. It's only natural.

CARLA. I know, but . . .

MARLENE. He'll be his old self tonight. Fix him a good supper and let him relax. Show him you love him. Cause you do . . .

CARLA. I know, but . . .

MARLENE. And you know you don't really want to leave.

CARLA. I swear I do, Marlene.

MARLENE. You always swear you do, but you don't. He's your husband and you belong here with him.

CARLA. I think he cares more about those dogs than he does Stacy and me.

MARLENE. Don't talk silly.

CARLA. I'm just so fed up with it all.

MARLENE. Oh, now . . .

CARLA. I haven't got any control. Everything keeps goin' round and round and things just keep happenin'. Comin' at me. I want everything to stop! So I can know what to do. So I can stop feelin' like . . . like there's somethin' else I should be doin'. I don't know. You now what I mean?

MARLENE. No, not really.

CARLA. Well, like you. You're happy. I'm so afraid if I don't leave, get away from here soon, I never will . . . I'll feel like this forever. Live the rest of my life wantin' instead of havin'.

MARLENE. Oh, don't think about it. I know how you are. You'll feel better once that mess is cleaned up.

CARLA. I told Larry I'd never take care of those dogs. And I mean it. I don't care how expensive they are or how many pedigrees and prizes they get. I ain't feedin' them, waterin' them, shovelin' their shit or cleanin' up their afterbirth. Never.

MARLENE. Alright. Alright. But you don't have to leave. Where were you plannin' on goin' anyway?

CARLA. I don't know.

MARLENE. How would you get there?

CARLA. I don't know. Guess that depends on where I was goin'. Right?

MARLENE. I suppose.

CARLA. Cyril says he'll drive me to Petersburg or someplace to catch a bus.

MARLENE. Bus to where? You can't run away. You ain't got no family, no friends. I'm the best friend you got, and I live here. (*beat*) What about money?

CARLA. What about it?

MARLENE. How much you got?

CARLA. I been savin'.

MARLENE. How much?

CARLA. I got about thirty-eight dollars.

MARLENE. I see.

CARLA. Well, Larry ain't give me any grocery money this week. I can't buy Stacy school clothes. She don't even have a pair of shoes that fit her anymore. I swear I don't know what he does with the money. I never see none of it.

MARLENE. You're really ready to leave. No money. Nobody. And no place to go. Carla Mae you're a mess. A wreck lookin' for a place to happen.

(*STACY comes out of the trailer dragging a suitcase and a grocery bag full of clothes. She is wearing her shoes.*)

STACY. I'm ready. When are we goin'? (*beat*)

MARLENE. Carla?

STACY. Mom?

MARLENE. You know you don't really want to leave. Stay here with me. This is where you belong.

STACY. Mom, are we goin' or not?

MARLENE. Stay. Ok?

CARLA. We ain't leavin' just yet.

STACY. I knew it.

CARLA. Be a little while till these clothes dry and I make up my mind where to go.

STACY. Sure.

CARLA. Leave your stuff inside. I'll let you know when we're leavin'.

MARLENE. Stacy, I think the boys are down at the creek lookin' for the pony. Why don't you go down there and help 'em?

STACY. Ok.

MARLENE. You tell 'em I said to be careful.

STACY. Ok. (*STACY exits.*)

CARLA. (*yelling after her*) Don't go too far 'case I get ready to leave. (*to MARLENE*) Thank goodness for Jimmie and Bobby or that poor child wouldn't have a soul in the world to play with her.

MARLENE. Yeah, they play together real good. Lord. Look what that crazy Cyril did. Crumpled up my brand new magazine. I ain't even read it yet. (*CARLA dumps the wash tub and takes it back into the trailer.*)

CARLA. Those silly boys. I still don't know where they got the idea there's a pony around here.

MARLENE. I don't either. They just decided it one day.

CARLA. They've spent the whole summer lookin' for it. There ain't no pony. Nothin' livin' around here for miles. (*MARLENE pages through her magazine studying some of the pictures as she talks with CARLA.*)

MARLENE. Big Jim encourages them. He bought them that durn bridle second hand. Guess he figures it gives 'em somethin' to do. (*holding up the magazine to CARLA*) You like that dress Cher's wearin'?

CARLA. It's ok.

MARLENE. I wouldn't wear it. You'd think with her money and bein' a mother, she'd dress better than that.

CARLA. A pony couldn't live here anyway. Nothin' to

eat. We've been here almost four years and I ain't seen a single blade of grass.

MARLENE. Shoot. Momma and Daddy never had any grass in their yard either. Every kid in Terre Haute use to come over and play in our yard. Killed all the grass. Momma didn't care though. I'm like her I guess, I'd rather look at kids than grass any day.

CARLA. They killed it all when they drove the bulldozers through here. Run a bulldozer through a burnt out stripper pit, string up a few 'lectric wires and call it a trailer court. This ain't a trailer court. It's a mud clearing stuck out here in the middle of nowhere. (*beat*)

MARLENE. Margeaux Hemmingway's eye brows bother me. She don't pluck 'em right. Too thick in the middle. You see? She should do them in more of an arch.

CARLA. I was goin' to plant grass when we first moved here and some bushes by the porch and a tree . . .

(*There is another explosion. The dogs howl.*)

CARLA. Shut up. Shut that up! I swear that's goin' to drive me crazy. Shut up! Every time they blast, those dogs go nuts. Dust everywhere. Coats everything. Even my neck is grimy.

MARLENE. Don't think about it.

CARLA. I can feel the grit.

MARLENE. You ought to be glad they're dynamitin'. Means they're about through. They dug down as far as they can go. Through the vein in some parts.

CARLA. Cyril said the high wall is over a hundred feet at his end.

MARLENE. Highest Big Jim's ever seen it on any job anywhere. Had a small slide the other day. Kind of scares me to think about them workin' next to that dirt wall. But at least they're above ground.

CARLA. They keep tearin' up, strippin' away. Everything dead and gray. Never grow nothin' here.

MARLENE. Don't think about it. We'll be movin' soon anyway.

CARLA. You think so?

MARLENE. Everything between Daylight and Boonville north's been stripped away. Ain't much coal left in Indiana.

CARLA. (*to herself*) Ain't much of anything.

MARLENE. When this pit runs out, it'll be time for us to move again.

CARLA. Where do you think we'll go this time?

MARLENE. Where ever the company sends them.

CARLA. Where you think?

MARLENE. West. Only strip minin' will be out west.

CARLA. What state?

MARLENE. Oh, I don't know.

CARLA. Texas?

MARLENE. Far west. Idaho. Montana . . .

CARLA. (*to herself*) Idaho . . .

MARLENE. Don't make much difference to me. Where ever the company says to go, we'll go. As long as we can go together and stay with the men, I don't care where it is.

CARLA. You ever think what would happen if they sent the men to different jobs?

MARLENE. They won't.

CARLA. They could.

MARLENE. We won't let 'em. We go together or we don't go at all. Company or no company, nothin' is goin' to separate us, Carla. That is if you don't pack up and leave me here.

(*MARLENE looks at CARLA for a moment. LOR-
ETTE enters. She carries a handful of socks, a sewing kit, a coffee cup and a pack of Camel
cigarettes.*)

LORETTE. Well, he got Grace.
MARLENE. What?
LORETTE. Grace Kelly.
MARLENE. Who?
LORETTE. Cary Grant. But he always gets the girl.
And he could have this old girl anytime he wants. He
can stick his dimpled chin in my trailer any time.
MARLENE. Lorette . . .
LORETTE. I get hot drawers just thinkin' about that
man. Him and Gary Cooper give me hot flashes all over
my wrinkled body.
MARLENE. You're plum nasty.
LORETTE. I know. And I love it too. (*to CARLA*)
You still here? I thought you'd be long gone by now.
CARLA. I haven't made up my mind.
LORETTE. No kidding?
MARLENE. She hasn't got any money.
LORETTE. She hasn't got any brains.
CARLA. Watch your mouth, Lorette.
LORETTE. Don't get your bowels in an uproar. Relax.
Carla, you got to learn if you don't like somethin', you
either change it or learn to live with it. But don't sit
around and bitch about it. Cause it gives me a headache.
(*LORETTE settles into her chair.*) Ohhhhh, me. I feel
like hard boiled shit today. Arthritis 'bout to kill me.
CARLA. Take more than arthritis, believe me.
(*LORETTE pulls out an envelope and fans herself.*)
LORETTE. It's hot today too. (*CARLA watches her
for a moment.*)

CARLA. Ok. We see it. You can put it away now.

LORETTE. What?

CARLA. Would you put that thing away? I get tired of lookin' at it.

LORETTE. Tough.

CARLA. You don't have to flaunt it. God knows we've seen it enough. We know you got money in there.

LORETTE. Well, you ain't seen *all* of it. (*LORETTE tosses the envelope on the table.*) Not just money any more. That is warm beaches. Cold beer. Palm trees. And the Gulf of Mexico. Right there.

CARLA. There's hundreds of dollars in here!

LORETTE. Nine hundred and thirty-two dollars.

CARLA. Where'd you get all this money?

LORETTE. Me and Charlie been savin' like hell, that's where. And we finally got enough saved for that down payment. Right here's the last of it.

MARLENE. That's wonderful.

CARLA. You never said nothin' about havin' this much money.

LORETTE. Carla Mae, there are talkers and doers. The doers do and don't talk. The talkers talk and don't do. You understand what I'm sayin'?

CARLA. Yes.

LORETTE. Good. Yeah, in another couple of years, when Charlie retires, we're goin' to move down there and live happily ever after. He's takin' off work a little early so we can go into Boonville and get a cashiers check and mail that sucker to the Gulf Breeze Condominiums in Clear Water, Florida. Clear . . . Water. Pretty name ain't it?

MARLENE. Beautiful. Sounds wonderful. (*beat*) What is a condominium?

LORETTE. It's like an apartment, except you own it

and you have someone else do all your house work and cut the grass.

MARLENE. That sounds nice.

LORETTE. All I'll have to do is lay around in my string bikini, drinkin' beer and playin' cards.

MARLENE. Is it right on the ocean?

LORETTE. Gulf of Mexico.

MARLENE. I read Burt Reynolds has got a dinner theatre down there somewhere.

LORETTE. You don't need no dinner theatre! Those condominiums are so luxurious, you never want to leave home. Ain't like a trailer. Besides they got cable TV . . . with Home Box Office. Perfect reception. Watch all the latest movies without commercial interruption right there on your own sun-filled patio.

CARLA. How do you know it's so nice?

LORETTE. It's the Sunshine State! An Ocean Paradise.

CARLA. I mean those condominiums.

LORETTE. What are you talkin' about? They're beautiful. Luxurious. Fully equipped. Maintenance free. Me and Charlie been readin' brochures like crazy. They got colored pictures and maps . . . I'll show you.

CARLA. You don't have to do that. We believe you.

LORETTE. Florida is beautiful. An Ocean Paradise. Maybe you could run off to Florida.

CARLA. Maybe. I might do that.

LORETTE. Go ahead. Nobody's stoppin' you. (*beat*)

CARLA. Let's do somethin'. What do you want to do?

MARLENE. Oh, I don't care. What do you want to do?

CARLA. I asked you.

LORETTE. We could bring my TV out here.

CARLA. I don't want to watch no TV.

LORETTE. There won't be another movie on till three thirty any way. THE FLAME AND THE ARROW. With Burt Lancaster and Virginia Mayo.

CARLA. Let's *do* somethin'. I'm sick of sittin' around her every day and every night doin' nothin'.

MARLENE. Wanna bake cookies for the kids?

CARLA. That's just what I want to do. Stand in my hot kitchen, ankle deep in afterbirth and bake cookies.

MARLENE. Use my kitchen.

CARLA. I do not want to bake cookies.

LORETTE. Who's afterbirth?

CARLA. Margaret had her pups in the trailer last night.

LORETTE. That's cute.

MARLENE. Here. You can read some of my magazines.

CARLA. I don't want that junk.

MARLENE. You don't have to read it. Just help me find a name.

CARLA. We goin' over that again? I thought you'd pick one by now.

MARLENE. Carla Mae, I only got two months. I gotta find one.

CARLA. You look for names. I already told you all the ones I know. I'll do my toenails. (*CARLA crosses to her suitcase and digs out a bottle of nail polish.*)

LORETTE. Don't mention toe nails. My old arthritic fingers can't take all this sewin'. Charlie has got the longest, sharpest, ugliest toe nails of any human being that ever wore out a pair of socks. Look at this. Reinforced toes. Wore this pair one time.

CARLA. Get him to clip them.

LORETTE. He won't do it.

CARLA. Why?

LORETTE. I don't know. I think somewhere way back in that hollow head of his, he's afraid if he cuts them he'll loose his strength or his pecker will fall off or somethin' . . . Every time he rolls over in bed he scratches me. I'm afraid my ankles are goin' to get infected. I told the man just cause he looks like a chicken doesn't mean he has to scratch like one.

CARLA. He doesn't look like a chicken.

LORETTE. Yes he does. Got that skinny neck and those sickly eyes . . .

CARLA. You exaggerate.

LORETTE. I do not. Charlie looks like a sick chicken. I don't know why I put up with him.

MARLENE. Hey! What about Farrah?

CARLA. What about her?

MARLENE. The name Farrah. Fare-ah! Like in Farrah Fawcett Majors.

CARLA. God, Marlene. I wouldn't name one of Larry's dogs that.

MARLENE. Why! It's a pretty name.

CARLA. Don't be ignorant. Nobody'd name their kid Farrah. Shit. Farrah? You better look for some boys' names while you're at it.

MARLENE. I don't need to.

CARLA. You might need to.

MARLENE. It's goin' to be a girl.

CARLA. How do you know?

MARLENE. Because I do. I know. With Jimmie and Bobby I got all bloated. Carried lots of water. My hands and feet swelled. Not the same this time. I can tell. It's a girl. It's got to be. Big Jim wants one really bad and I'm goin' to give him a little girl.

CARLA. I don't care what Big Jim wants. You gotta take what you get.

MARLENE. It's goin' to be a girl! (*several beats*) Two miscarriages tore Big Jim up pretty bad. When I had to stay in the hospital that last time, he got real upset. That's why we didn't try for so long. But we talked it over and he decided we wanted to try again for a little girl. This is Big Jim's little girl. And I got to find a name for her.

CARLA. What if Big Jim wanted a monkey? Would you have that?

MARLENE. What are you talkin' about?

CARLA. You always do what he says.

MARLENE. I do not.

CARLA. Do too.

MARLENE. You know I don't.

CARLA. You do everything he says.

MARLENE. He's right most of the time. But I don't always do what he says. We fight like cats and dogs.

CARLA. Not like me and Larry do.

MARLENE. Yeah, we do. Use to fight anyway. Don't fight much now, but we use to fight . . .

LORETTE. Me and Charlie never fight. He knows there'd only be two hits. When I hit him. And he hits the floor.

CARLA. Ain't nobody in the world fight like me and Larry.

MARLENE. You wanna bet?

CARLA. I'd bet anything.

MARLENE. This one time, before the kids were born, Big Jim was workin' construction before goin' to work for the company. And we were rentin' a little furnished house. I worked all day gettin' the house all cleaned up. Baked cookies. Did the wash. It was one of those days. I use to do a lot more of that stuff than I do now. Anyway, I was beat. So, I sit down on the couch and propped my feet up on the coffee table and started readin' my magazines. Well, Big Jim comes home from work mad as hell at this young, cocky foreman he's workin' for. So he takes it out on me. He had stopped and had a few beers and picked up a six pack on his way home. And he walks in and wants to know why I've got my feet propped up on the good coffee table. I told him not to worry about it. It was rented. And he said, "Don't talk back. Take your feet down off the table". I said no. And he said you better. And I said you take them down for me. And he said, "Like hell!" And he yanked that table out from under my feet, went to the front door and threw the coffee table right out into the middle of the front yard. I didn't say a word. I got up, grabbed his six pack and walked over and threw it right out in the front yard. Big Jim didn't say nothin'. He walked over, unplugged the floor lamp and tossed it out. So I grabbed the two wedding pictures off the wall and threw them out. He threw out the chair and I threw out all the toss pillows off the couch. We just kept throwin'. Never said a word. More we threw out, the madder we got. Finally, we got to the couch and it took both of us to throw it out. By the time we emptied the living room, we were both so tired we just stood there on the front porch tryin' to catch our breath. Then we looked at one another and I laughed. And he laughed. We both started laughin', said to hell with it. Left everything in the yard and went up to bed. And that's the secret.

CARLA. What?

MARLENE. Don't ever go to bed angry.

LORETTE. She'd never go to bed.

CARLA. You're right. I'm pissed off at Larry ninety percent of the time.

MARLENE. Carla Mae, don't talk like that. He's your husband, the man you married.

CARLA. No. He ain't the man I married. He may have the same name, but he ain't the same man. He's different. Sloppy. Out of shape. Big ol' beer gut hangin' over his belt buckle. That ain't the man I married. (*BOBBY dashes up and goes inside the trailer.*)

MARLENE. (*to BOBBY*) Don't slam the door. (*The door slams. Back to the women.*) They all change once they get married. It's nothin' new.

LORETTE. Charlie hasn't changed. (*beat*) Damnit.

MARLENE. Big Jim has changed a lot . . . But I think it's for the best.

CARLA. Larry use to be in good shape. Built! Summer before my senior year in high school, I was seventeen years old workin' as a carhop at the Dog-N-Suds, when Larry pulled in drivin' an orange GTO with a black racin' stripe. The back end jacked up. Conway Twitty blarin' on his tape deck. Singin' "It's Only Make Believe". I 'bout dropped a tray full of hot dogs. Mouth fell open. I thought he was a god in a chariot.

LORETTE. He's still a pretty good hunk. (*BOBBY comes out of the trailer with a plastic bag full of carrots.*)

MARLENE. What have you got?

BOBBY. Carrots.

MARLENE. Why?

BOBBY. For the trap.

MARLENE. Trap? What kind of trap?

BOBBY. For the pony. We need carrots for bait.

MARLENE. Well you don't need a whole bag. One is enough. Put the rest away.

BOBBY. We need at least four.

MARLENE. One.

BOBBY. Three?

MARLENE. Two.

BOBBY. Right. (*BOBBY goes back inside.*)

CARLA. He was older too. Just back from Nam. Had lots of money, wore his combat boots and a brand new pair of skin-tight Levis he got at the PX. I didn't even mind his short hair. I walked over to where he was leanin' against his GTO smokin' a cigarette and I asked him if I could help him. And he kinda flicked the ashes and said, "I sure hope so." I got his order and we talked. He told me about Viet Nam and said he wanted to show me his scar sometime. Have I told you about that?

LORETTE. Many times. (*BOBBY runs out of the trailer with the two carrots and exits.*)

MARLENE. (*calling after BOBBY*) You be careful.

BOBBY. We will.

CARLA. He was so lucky. Right there. Big ol' ugly scar. Right there on his left leg. Another couple of inches and . . . good bye family jewels. That land mine killed the two boys in front of him. He told me he felt he was the luckiest man in the world. Not because he didn't die, but because he could still have sex.

LORETTE. My kinda man.

CARLA. Jealous! Talk about bein' jealous. One night, before I got off work, Mary Lucy Tury asked Larry to take her for a ride in his GTO. Well, I beat that bitch over the head with a mug full of root beer. About killed her. Lost my job. But I didn't care, cause I had all I wanted . . . Larry and that GTO. I told him I'd kill him if I ever caught him with another woman. I still would today. If I even thought it, I'd leave in a minute!

LORETTE. Carla, you're gettin' froggy again. Relax. Help Marlene find a name.

CARLA. Hell, go ahead and name her Farrah.

MARLENE. No. You don't like it.

LORETTE. Name her Greta or . . . Gregory Peck. Call her Greggie.

MARLENE. Oh, Lorette . . .

CARLA. Do like I did. Ask one of the nurses in the delivery room.

MARLENE. You didn't do that!

CARLA. Sure I did. That's how I named Stacy.

MARLENE. You can't just name a girl anything. Boys you can name about anything. They always end up with nicknames anyway. So it don't make any difference. But a girl! That's her identity. How she knows who she is. What makes her unique. I don't want her to have a typical name. I want her to be unique.

LORETTE. Name her Telephone.

MARLENE. Telephone?

LORETTE. It's got a nice ring to it. (*CARLA falls out of her chair laughing.*)

MARLENE. It ain't a jokin' matter. Think about it. What would of happened if Farrah had not been named Farrah Fawcett Majors? You ever thought about that? She's got the perfect name for herself. Not Juanita Fawcett Majors, or Carol Fawcett Majors. But Farrah Fawcett Majors! She's unique. She never should of dropped the Majors from her name when she and Lee got separated. Just ruins it. Farrah Fawcett. Don't sound right without the Majors. All in the name.

CARLA. Alright. Name her Farrah.

MARLENE. No. You don't like it. You're goin' to be her godmother, so I want you to like the name I pick.

CARLA. What so you want to do? Besides look for names.

LORETTE. I got my cards. We could . . .

CARLA. No thank you.

MARLENE. Want me to make some lemonade? It's just frozen, but it's cold.

CARLA. I don't want any.

LORETTE. Me either.

CARLA. Tell you what I want. I want to go to a beauty parlor. Can't remember the last time I got my hair cut. Feel like a pioneer stuck out here. Ratt-ass mess. Ends so ragged, looks like one of the dogs chewed them off. I think it's turnin' gray. Twenty-six years old and I got a headful of gray hair.

MARLENE. It ain't gray. If you wanna see gray hair, look here. Now that's gray.

LORETTE. I don't know what you two are worried about. I'm goin' bald. Me and Charlie both. He's losin' it in front and I'm losin' it in back. Another couple of years, we'll look like brothers.

CARLA. I got just as much gray hair as she does and I ain't near as old.

MARLENE. Well, thanks!

CARLA. You know what I mean.

MARLENE. Uh huh.

CARLA. I didn't mean it like that.

MARLENE. Nine years ain't that much older. Thirty-five ain't antique.

CARLA. I know. But you seem older.

MARLENE. Thanks.

CARLA. Oh, you know what I mean. Guess cause you're pregnant and because you mother everybody makes you seem older. But you don't look it. Really!

MARLENE. Yes, I do.

CARLA. No, you don't.

MARLENE. Carla Mae, it doesn't bother me. I don't think about it. But if your gray hair bothers you, get yourself to a salon.

CARLA. How'd I get there?

LORETTE. Wanda gets her hair done every Thursday. Go with her.

CARLA. I'd let my hair turn green, rot off and fall out on the ground before I got in a car with her. She only gets her hair done cause she's a whore. It's true. Whore hair! I don't like it at all. Looks like a football helmet.

MARLENE. I like the way she's got it now.

CARLA. It's ugly old helmet hair.

LORETTE. I'd rather have her helmet than my bald spot.

CARLA. She use to not get her hair done every week. She looked like warmed over dog shit most of the time. Didn't start fixin' herself up till . . . till after Darrel got electrocuted. It's the truth! He wasn't in the ground three days and she got her hair done. Within a week, she started sellin' groceries and beer out of her trailer. Screwin' everybody.

MARLENE. Carla.

CARLA. She does it for money. I know. Hell yes, I could get my hair done every week too if I was a big time business whore.

MARLENE. I think you're jealous.

CARLA. What!

MARLENE. You're jealous of her.

CARLA. Don't make me laugh. Why would I be jealous?

MARLENE. Cause Wanda does what she wants. She comes and goes as she pleases. Doesn't have to answer to nobody and you're jealous.

CARLA. Jealous? Just cause she gets her hair done every week and I have to get the dogs to chew mine off. (*The three women laugh at CARLA'S absurd remark. LORETTE, as always, begins coughing when she laughs. CARLA begins to comb her hair.*)

MARLENE. You're a mess.

CARLA. (*indicating a mirror.*) Hold that for me, would you?

MARLENE. Sure. (*beat*) Who have you seen over there?

CARLA. What?

MARLENE. Over at Wanda's. Who have you seen over there?

CARLA. I ah . . . don't know. I think Freddie Johnson, but I really . . .

LORETTE. (*interrupting*) Hey, you want to see somethin' that will really make you jealous . . . (*She coughs.*)

CARLA. (*to MARLENE*) Hold that up a little higher.

LORETTE. I'll grab some of those brochures. I'm goin' to the trailer . . .

MARLENE. You don't have to do that.

LORETTE. I'm out of cigarettes anyway. I want you to see those condominiums. Knock your eyes out. (*LORETTE starts to leave, but remembers the envelope and takes it from the table.*) The envelope, please. Can I get anybody anything?

MARLENE. No. I think I'll go in and make some lemonade. Hot enought. We could use it.

LORETTE. Be back shortly (*LORETTE exits.*)

CARLA. I never been to Florida.

MARLENE. Me neither.

CARLA. Bet you it's nice.

MARLENE. (*starting inside*) Those condominiums sound like they'd be real nice.

CARLA. Probably a lot of opportunities in Florida. Wonder if I could get a job down there?

MARLENE. I wouldn't know. I never been south at all . . . (*MARLENE has started up the concrete block steps to her trailer, but stops and holds her side.*) Ohhh, Lord.

CARLA. Marlene?

MARLENE. (*recovering*) Ahhh . . .

CARLA. You alright?

MARLENE. Yes.

CARLA. Here. Sit down.

MARLENE. Ahhh, she is restless. I'm ok, Carla. Really, I'm fine. She's never kicked like that before.

CARLA. You want to sit down?

MARLENE. No. I'm fine. (*to the baby*) Settle down. You hear me? (*to CARLA*) If somethin' happened to this baby, I don't know what Big Jim would do.

CARLA. Sure you're ok?

MARLENE. Yeah. Shoot. I'll fix that lemonade. It's frozen, but it's all I got.

(*MARLENE starts toward her trailer. WANDA enters. WANDA has jet black hair that is neatly combed in a somewhat dated style. She is tall and lean and wears new designer jeans, sandals and a halter top.*)

WANDA. Hey, Marlene. (*pause*) Marlene?

MARLENE. Huh? Oh, hi Wanda. How are you?

WANDA. Hot. Somethin' wrong?

MARLENE. No. Nothin's wrong. (*WANDA starts to speak to CARLA, but she decides against it.*)

WANDA. How's the baby, Marlene?

MARLENE. Restless.

WANDA. Not going to be too much longer and you can dump your load. Got a name for it yet?

MARLENE. No. I'm still lookin'.

WANDA. I told you, if it's a girl, name her Wanda Jean.

CARLA. (*to herself*) Hummph . . . (*WANDA shoots a look to CARLA.*)

WANDA. And if it's a boy Darrel Lamar.

MARLENE. Well . . .

WANDA. What are the boys up to?

MARLENE. They're down by the creek . . .

WANDA. Some fellas aren't they? I believe they're goin' to be as handsome as their daddy. How is Big Jim anyway?

MARLENE. Fine.

WANDA. I ain't seen him lately. I don't ever see him. He must be real busy.

MARLENE. Yeah. He's been puttin' in a lot of overtime. He don't even come home for lunch any more. (*pause*) Listen, I was goin' in for some lemonade. You want a glass?

WANDA. No. I'm on my way into Evansville to pick up a few things at K-Mart. Just wanted to see if you needed anything.

CARLA. (*to herself*) She'll charge you double if she does.

WANDA. Wrong. Since I'm making the trip, I figured if there is anything you wanted I could pick it up for you.

MARLENE. You could pick up a new Enquirer for me if you would.

WANDA. Be more than glad to.

MARLENE. Here, let me go in and get you some money.

WANDA. No, I'll get it. You can pay me when I get back.

MARLENE. There's no big hurry is there? Why don't you have one glass of lemonade? (*WANDA checks her watch.*)

WANDA. Ok, sure. I got a little time yet. (*MARLENE goes into the trailer. WANDA turns to CARLA. Silence. Finally . . .*)

WANDA. Hot today ain't it?

CARLA. I ought to bash in your face.

WANDA. You ain't talked to me for over two months and that's the first words that come out of your mouth?

CARLA. You're sickening.

WANDA. What is wrong with you?

CARLA. Sick-en-ing!

WANDA. Why do you hate me?

CARLA. So sweet you're sickening.

WANDA. What!

CARLA. Do you have to rub her nose in it?

WANDA. What are you talking about?

CARLA. You know damn well what I'm talkin' about.

WANDA. I don't have any idea. I can't read your tiny, little mind.

CARLA. Don't get smart with me. And don't play dumb.

WANDA. I think this heat has boiled your brain.

CARLA. Nothin' of mine's boiled. I know what's goin' on. I'm on to your little game.

WANDA. What game?

CARLA. I don't even want to talk about it. Makes me sick.

WANDA. No. What game?

CARLA. The one you're playin' with Big Jim! (*several beats*)

WANDA. Me and Big Jim ain't playing nothing.

CARLA. I know . . .

WANDA. Nothing!

CARLA. I know. She don't know. But I do know.

WANDA. You don't know what you're talking about.

CARLA. I know. Just leave it at that. I know.

WANDA. You been out here too long. You don't know anything. The sun has boiled your brain. Your brains are boiled . . .

(*CYRIL enters on the tail end of WANDA'S line.*)

CYRIL. Sun boiled whose brain?

WANDA. Yours!

CYRIL. Mine?

WANDA. Yes, yours. Shorty.

CYRIL. No, sir. Can't boil my brains. On hot days I take them out and leave 'em in a shoe box under my bed. Right under . . . (*CYRIL senses the tension between the two women.*) . . . the bed. (*beat*) Well! (*beat*) Here we are. Two of my most favorite girls in the world.

WANDA. How's your hand?

CYRIL. Huh?

WANDA. Still throbbing?

CYRIL. You mean the hand I severely injured in a freak mining accident that causes me great pain and suffering, which I endure with manly courage?

WANDA. Yes.

CYRIL. It's fine.

CARLA. You get your cigarettes, Cyril?

CYRIL. Yep. Sure did. Right here. Fresh pack of Pall Mall.

WANDA. By the way Cyril, you left these over in my trailer.

CYRIL. What?

WANDA. Thought you might want your panties back. (*WANDA pulls out the panties CYRIL wore earlier from her purse.*)

CYRIL. Wanda!

CARLA. Give those here.

WANDA. No . . .

CARLA. Give those to me.

WANDA. No. They're Cyril's

CARLA. Damnit, give 'em to me.

WANDA. I can't . . .

CYRIL. Now girls.

WANDA. . . . they're Cyril's.

CARLA. They are mine!

CYRIL. Girls!

WANDA. Yours!

CARLA. Give 'em to me.

WANDA. Oh, I see . . .

CARLA. You don't see shit. Give me those pants. (*CARLA grabs the panties. There follows a tug-of-war between the two women.*)

WANDA. Don't grab like that!

CARLA. I'll grab what I want.

WANDA. Let go.

CARLA. Make me. (*CYRIL jerks the panties away from both of them.*)

CYRIL. Now girls! Let's not fight over the panties. They are mine. Finders-Keepers. They belong to me now, so there's nothin' to argue about . . . (*CYRIL pulls the panties over his head and wears them like a hat.*) Perfect fit! Sit down. And don't fuss. It makes my hand hurt. Sit down. (*WANDA and CARLA relax their stances but the tension still remains.*) Well . . . You think wearin' panties on my head will make me crotchety? (*MARLENE enters from her trailer carrying a tray with three glasses and a pitcher of lemonade.*) Hey, good lookin'! What you got cookin'! Here come the prettiest pregnant woman I've seen all day. Let me take that for you.

MARLENE. What are you doin' with those on your head?

CYRIL. Just had my hair done. No seriously. It prevents sun stroke. You sit down and let me pour you a big glass of lemonade. That's what it is ain't it?

MARLENE. It's frozen . . .

CYRIL. Lemonade! Made by an old maid with a spade in the shade . . . or somethin' like that. You rest yourself and that baby and I'll pour you some. Here we are.

MARLENE. Thanks.

CYRIL. Drinks for everybody. (*CYRIL passes out the poured lemonade.*) This is fun. I like bein' off work. Here with you women. (*There is an explosion of dynamite. The dogs bark and howl.*) Boom! Hey, dogs! Quiet down. Man they are really goin' at it. (*to the women*) Hey! You know why coal miners make better lovers? (*beat*) They dig deeper. (*CYRIL laughs, but none of the women react.*) Well . . . This is fun. What'll we talk about? What do women talk about?

MARLENE. Men.

WANDA. Other women.

CARLA. You.

CYRIL. Me? No. I ain't worth talkin' about. Come on now. Pretend I'm one of the girls. Treat me like one of the girls.

WANDA. That could be dangerous.

(*LORETTE enters carrying a handful of brochures and pamphlets and a fresh pack of Camel cigarettes.*)

CYRIL. Wait a minute! Here she comes . . . (*sings*) Miss America!

LORETTE. What's he doin' here?

MARLENE. Pretendin' he's one of the girls.

LORETTE. (*looks at the panties on CYRIL'S head*) I see he's dressed for it.

CYRIL. Lorette, you get prettier everyday.

LORETTE. Go to hell.

CYRIL. You know you don't mean that. I'm your favorite boy . . .

LORETTE. Cyril, I wouldn't piss on you if you were on fire.

CYRIL. You sweet talkin' thing. Come here and have some lemonade.

LORETTE. I don't want any. Here's those brochures. Feast you eyes on paradise. (*She tossed them on the table.*)

WANDA. Hi.

LORETTE. How are you?

WANDA. Hot.

CYRIL. What are these?

MARLENE. Condominiums. They're like apartments, except you don't cut the grass.

CYRIL. I don't see any grass to cut. Just a lot of sand a big lake.

LORETTE. That is the Gulf of Mexico you goof ass.

CYRIL. Oh.

LORETTE. I swear if you had a brain it'd be lonesome.

CYRIL. But I'm happy.

MARLENE. It's where Charlie and Lorette are gonna retire. (*to Wanda*) Where are you goin' when the work's through here?

WANDA. More than likely Illinois. I think I got a good deal on a little truck stop and twenty-four hour grocery right outside Joliet. My brother-in-law found it. Might go in partners with him. What about you, Cyril.

CYRIL. I don't know. Where ever the company sends me I'll go. Kankakee. Tennessee. Long as I'm free makes no difference to me . . . I just do what I'm told. Probably go west with everyone else. Follow you, Lorette.

LORETTE. I'd rather have stretch marks.

WANDA. How are Margaret's pups?

MARLENE. Carla?

CARLA. What?

MARLENE. She asked you about the pups.

CARLA. They're ok.

MARLENE. They're real cute, Wanda.

WANDA. I love little puppies.

MARLENE. They're in the trailer.

WANDA. (*to LORETTE*) You want to see them?

LORETTE. No, I don't want to see a bunch of stinkin' puppies.

WANDA. I want to see them. (*WANDA starts for the trailer.*)

CARLA. You can't.

WANDA. I just want to peek.

CARLA. Nobody can see them.

CYRIL. She can look.

CARLA. No.

MARLENE. She won't touch 'em. She just wants to look.

CARLA. I said nobody can see them. Larry don't want nobody botherin' his dogs.

WANDA. I won't bother them.

CARLA. I said no.

WANDA. (*going to the trailer*) I just want to look at . . .

CARLA. Don't step inside that trailer!

WANDA. Why!

CARLA. Cause I don't want a whore inside my house.

CYRIL. Carla!

LORETTE. Don't talk like . . .

MARLENE. Apologize.

CARLA. Go to hell.

MARLENE. I'm sorry, Wanda . . .

CARLA. Don't apologize to her!

MARLENE. I will . . .

CARLA. Not to her.

WANDA. That's alright. I just wanted to see the puppies. If Carla doesn't want me to, that's quite alright. It's just such a shame about the one puppy dying. Margaret getting scared and yanking out its guts.

CARLA. Who told you?

WANDA. What?

CARLA. About the dead pup. Who told you?

CYRIL. What dead pup?

WANDA. Larry, of course.

CARLA. When? When'd he tell you?

WANDA. Last night.

CARLA. When?

WANDA. After you went to bed. He came over and bought some beer from me.

CARLA. I didn't know nothin' about that.

WANDA. Carla, there's a lot of things you don't know about.

CARLA. Like what!

CYRIL. Go lots of lemonade here!

WANDA. I've got to go. Marlene, I'll pick up your Enquirer.

MARLENE. Thanks.

WANDA. Carla, you want me to pick up some Vitamin E for Larry.

CARLA. What for?

WANDA. I hear Vitamin E is real good for scars. (*CARLA lunges at WANDA. CYRIL struggles to keep them apart and still protect his hand.*)

CARLA. Bitch!

MARLENE. Carla . . .

CARLA. Dirty Bitch Whore!

LORETTE. Cyril stop . . .

CARLA. I'll kill you!

CYRIL. Calm Down!

CARLA. Bash in your ugly face. Whore!

LORETTE. Marlene, get back! You'll get hurt. (*CYRIL manages to separate the two women. He holds CARLA.*)

WANDA. Get back . . .

CYRIL. Wanda, you better get out of here.

LORETTE. What is goin' on?

CYRIL. I can't hold her forever.

CARLA. Run you whore . . .

CYRIL. Shut up! (*WANDA exits.*)

CARLA. I'll kill you, you ever come 'round me again.

LORETTE. Marlene, you alright?

MARLENE. Yes.

CARLA. Bitch!

MARLENE. Carla, she's gone.

CARLA. Whore . . .

MARLENE. She's gone. Quit actin' so childish.

CARLA. (*to CYRIL*) Let me go.

CYRIL. I'm not lettin' you go till you quiet down.

CARLA. You're hurtin' my arm.

CYRIL. Calm down.

CARLA. Let go of me.

CYRIL. Calm down and I will.

CARLA. I am calmed down.

MARLENE. Let her go.

CARLA. That's it. I'm leavin'. I'm not stayin' here another second.

MARLENE. Carla . . .

CARLA. Cyril, you promised you'd drive me. By damn, you keep your word. Staaaaaaccccceeee!

MARLENE. She means it, Cyril.

CARLA. You promised you'd drive me.

CYRIL. I will. Where do you want to go?

CARLA. Out of here. Anywhere!

MARLENE. Carla, if you're really goin' . . .

CARLA. If! There's no if about it. Staacceee!

MARLENE. Then go to Momma and Daddy's in Terre Haute. I'll give you the address . . .

CYRIL. That's a pretty long drive.

MARLENE. It's not that far. I'll call and let them know you need a few days to think things over.

CARLA. I've done my thinkin'. Staaccee! (*The three children run up to the trailers while playing tag.*)

STACY. What!

CARLA. Get over here. Grab your things . . .

(*There is a thunderous explosion. Everyone stops. There is a second explosion that is louder than the first. CYRIL drops the suitcase he is holding. The dogs bark and howl. MARLENE, CARLA and LORETTE remain frozen for several seconds.*)

CYRIL. (*under his breath*) No . . .

(*In the background, JIMMIE grabs his heart and falls to the ground. The other children giggle.*)

JIMMIE. Got me!

MARLENE. Oh, my God.

CARLA. What was that?

BOBBY. (*falling down*) Boooooom!

CYRIL. I don't know.

MARLENE. God, no . . .

(*STACY also falls to the ground. The children continue laughing and falling to the ground. The dogs howl.*)

CYRIL. I'll find out . . .

CARLA. I'm goin' with you.

CYRIL. Stay here!

CARLA. I want . . .

CYRIL. All of you stay here! I'll come back and let you know what happened. But stay right here. (*CYRIL runs off. The three women look at one another in silence as the lights fade to black.*)

END OF ACT I

ACT TWO

The lights come up. MARLENE is paging through a magazine, while LORETTE plays cards. US., CARLA stands with her back to the audience looking off in the direction of the stripper pits. The suitcases are still packed and in view. The lemonade and glasses have been struck. The children are playing a game of Hide-N-Seek. STACY stands at the gas tank with her eyes covered and counting.

STACY. 80! 81, 82, 83, 84 . . . (*JIMMIE and BOBBY scurry off to find hiding places.*) 90! 91, 92, 93, 94, 95, 96, 97 . . . 98 . . . 99 . . . 100! Ready or not, here I come . . . (*STACY looks for the boys. CARLA crosses to the women.*)

CARLA. We should of told the kids.

MARLENE. Told them what? We don't know anything yet.

CARLA. They should know . . .

MARLENE. Don't bother them. They're better off not knowin' anything. Just let 'em play.

LORETTE. (*to CARLA*) It's your turn. (*CARLA goes back to the cards. JIMMIE dashes up and tags base, which happens to be the gas tank. STACY goes offstage to look for BOBBY.*)

JIMMIE. Home Free!

CARLA. It's been almost two hours. We should of heard somethin' by now.

MARLENE. We will.

CARLA. When?

MARLENE. I don't know.

CARLA. When do you think?

MARLENE. You keep askin' me that . . . I don't know.

CARLA. We should go over there and find out.

MARLENE. We got no business over there.

CARLA. No business!

MARLENE. There's nothin' we can do.

CARLA. We could do somethin' . . .

MARLENE. Don't think about it.

CARLA. Anything's better than nothin'.

MARLENE. Don't think about it!

LORETTE. Come on. Come on, you two. Cyrill'll be back soon. He'll let us know what happened. Probably wasn't anything serious or we would have heard somethin' by now.

MARLENE. You think so?

LORETTE. We haven't heard the whistle. They ain't give any kind of signal . . .

CARLA. It's been too quiet over there.

LORETTE. If you don't hear the whistle, it's nothin' serious.

CARLA. Maybe it wasn't the pits. Could of been a test or something . . .

LORETTE. Come on, play cards.

CARLA. Whose turn is it?

LORETTE. Yours. Draw. (*LORETTE coughs.*) Ah, hell . . . (*She coughs again.*)

CARLA. Lorette, that sounds terrible. You smoke too much.

LORETTE. No, I don't. I cough too much.

MARLENE. Carol Burnette's aged well, ain't she? (*MARLENE holds up the magazine.*)

LORETTE. Yeah, I've always like her. (*indicating her cards*) Rummy!

(*STACY chases BOBBY behind one of the trailers.*)

STACY. (*offstage*) Bobby, I found you. You're it!

BOBBY. (*offstage*) No I'm not . . . (*BOBBY dashes to the gas tank, then runs offstage.*) Home Free!

MARLENE. (*to herself*) Carol. Caroline . . . Courtney.

CARLA. Huh?

MARLENE. Oh, nothin'. I was just . . . Courtney! You like that name? Courtney.

CARLA. Naw. Sounds too . . . cute.

MARLENE. Yeah, you're right.

LORETTE. When I was a secretary, I worked with a girl named Courtney. Cute girl.

CARLA. See.

LORETTE. Dumb as a rock. She use to forget where she was goin'. Get up from her desk, start across the room with a handful of papers and all of a sudden she'd stop. Stand there in the middle of the floor with a blank look on her face. Didn't know which way to go. (*LORETTE laughs at the memory.*) Ol' dumb Courtney. She's one of the reasons I started smokin'. Hell, that was over twenty years ago.

CARLA. Were you married then?

LORETTE. No, it was right after my divorce.

CARLA. Which one?

LORETTE. My second. And last.

CARLA. You sure knew how to pick 'em, didn't you?

LORETTE. Oh, it wasn't that. They were both pretty nice fellas. The first one, Nicky, I was seventeen when I married him. He was a handsome son of a gun. But that's all he was. I got bored and left him real quick. The second one . . . it's your draw . . . the second one, he was a really nice guy. Married to him almost eight years.

He gave me about anything I wanted. New clothes, a TV, car of my own . . . But I got bored again. So, I packed up the kids and everything I could cram into the car. Ran off to Marion.

CARLA. Kentucky?

LORETTE. Illinois. You see. I was sure there was somethin' bigger and better. And I was goin' to find it. So I got me an apartment and a job workin' as a secretary with dumb Courtney. Kept busy and fooled myself into thinkin' it was what I wanted. But I wasn't happy. After a while I realized, of course by then it was too late, but I realized it wasn't them I was tryin' to run away from. It was me. (*pause*) Funny thing was, as soon as I understood that, every day got a little better, 'till I was actually feelin' pretty good about myself. Then I met Charlie . . . the Chicken. Whose turn is it anyway?

CARLA. Yours.

MARLENE. You and Charlie never had kids.

LORETTE. Nope.

MARLENE. Why?

LORETTE. Never needed them. A boy from the first marriage, two girls from the second, I figured that was enough for anybody.

MARLENE. You don't see 'em much.

LORETTE. I know.

CARLA. In fact you never see 'em.

LORETTE. Carla, play your cards.

MARLENE. Are they still in Marion?

LORETTE. Far as I know.

MARLENE. You're not sure!

LORETTE. (*to CARLA*) It's your draw.

MARLENE. But, they're your children.

LORETTE. I know that.

CARLA. How come you never see 'em?

LORETTE. Carla, come on. Play the damn cards.

MARLENE. How come they don't visit you?

LORETTE. They won't do it. Haven't seen 'em or talked to 'em . . . in a long time. (*beat*) I've got a couple of grand-children I've never seen. Hell, they don't even send me Christmas cards.

MARLENE. Why not? (*beat*) Lorette?

LORETTE. Ohhhhh . . . They resent me and Charlie 'cause we never got married.

CARLA. What!

MARLENE. You didn't!

LORETTE. We never got around to it.

MARLENE. You're not married?

LORETTE. No. Well, yes. Legally I guess we are. Common Law. But we never actually got married. Kids resent that. Think I'm an old floozy livin' in sin . . .

MARLENE. I never knew. I assumed you were.

LORETTE. You assumed? Hell, I assumed. Everyone assumed . . . except the kids. After nineteen years with someone, you assume. (*beat*)

CARLA. (*teasing her*) You adultress hussy!

LORETTE. Oh, shut up and play cards.

(*JIMMIE, BOBBY and STACY run up to the women.*)

STACY. Momma?

CARLA. What?

STACY. I want to show Jimmie and Bobby the puppies.

JIMMIE. (*to MARLENE*) Can we see the puppies?

CARLA. (*to STACY*) Where are your shoes?

MARLENE. (*to JIMMIE*) You'll have to ask Carla.

STACY. I don't know.

CARLA. Don't know. What do you mean you don't know? Where are they?

STACY. Down at the creek.

CARLA. You march right down there and get those shoes and bring them up here.

STACY. Ohhhh . . .

CARLA. Now! (*STACY exits.*)

BOBBY. Carla, can we see the puppies?

JIMMIE. Can we?

MARLENE. What you say?

JIMMIE. Please.

BOBBY. Please, Carla. Please?

CARLA. Ok. But don't touch 'em. Their eyes ain't even open yet. Margaret might bite you if you touch 'em.

BOBBY. We won't.

CARLA. And be quiet.

BOBBY. We will.

CARLA. Ok.

JIMMIE. Come on. (*The two boys start for the trailer, but BOBBY suddenly stops and comes back to CARLA.*)

BOBBY. Thanks, Carla. (*BOBBY quickly turns and goes inside with JIMMIE.*)

MARLENE. I love them to death. My little men. Big Jim calls them his little men. But they're my little men.

CARLA. Your little men better be careful. Margaret can be mean if you bother her puppies.

MARLENE. They'll be quiet. (*CARLA crosses us. and looks off for a moment.*)

CARLA. What if it was the highwall?

MARLENE. It wasn't.

CARLA. What if it blew?

MARLENE. It didn't.

CARLA. How do you know?

MARLENE. It didn't. (*STACY runs up and places her shoes on the table.*)

CARLA. You got mud on them.

STACY. I now. That's why I took them off.

CARLA. You're cleanin' them up.

STACY. (*taking the shoes*) I want to see the puppies, too.

CARLA. Ok. But you leave them on the porch, cause you're goin' to clean and polish them after while.

STACY. I will. (*STACY goes inside the trailer.*)

CARLA. God, I wish Larry'd give me some money so I could but that kid another pair of shoes and some school clothes. She's outgrown everything.

MARLENE. Her clothes would be perfect for hand me downs.

CARLA. What's that suppose to mean?

MARLENE. When you goin' to have another one?

CARLA. Another what?

MARLENE. Baby.

CARLA. Huh?

MARLENE. A baby. Don't you think it's about time for Stacy to have a baby sister? No. A baby brother!

CARLA. If she wants one, she can find her own.

MARLENE. You should talk to Larry and get pregnant.

LORETTE. That's not how you do it, Marlene.

MARLENE. You know what I'm sayin'. Talk it over. Larry told Jim he'd love a son.

CARLA. I'll leave the baby makin' to you.

MARLENE. It's what you need. A little boy . . .

CARLA. You made your point . . .

MARLENE. If you started now, you could have it by next spring.

CARLA. Don't push it! (*beat*) Ok?
MARLENE. It was only a suggestion.
CARLA. I know. Let's just drop it.

(*BOBBY, JIMMIE and STACY come out of the trailer.*)

BOBBY. (*overlapping with JIMMIE*) They're cute!
JIMMIE. They got little, tiny ears . . .
BOBBY. She's got five puppies.
JIMMIE. Five of them!
BOBBY. They're all asleep.
JIMMIE. Their eyes are closed . . .
BOBBY. And they're smilin' . . . Like this. (*BOBBY shows MARLENE how the puppies look when asleep.*)
STACY. Margaret needs some water.
CARLA. So?
STACY. She's thirsty.
CARLA. You give her some. I ain't givin' her any. (*STACY gets a water bowl, fills it and carries it into the trailer, then returns to the porch to listen to MARLENE.*)
JIMMIE. The puppies all have little strings.
MARLENE. Strings? Where?
JIMMIE. On their bellies.
BOBBY. They hang down from their bellies.
MARLENE. That's their cord.
JIMMIE. Wha . . .
BOBBY. What's that?
MARLENE. Their cords. When they were inside their momma's belly, that's how she feeds 'em. They're in a little sack, asleep. And the momma feeds them through the cord.
JIMMIE. Huh?

MARLENE. It's sort of like a tube that shoots food from her belly into the puppy's belly.

BOBBY. (*truly amazed*) Gaaaahhhh . . .

MARLENE. When the puppies are born the cord is not needed anymore. So the mother chews if off or someone cuts it off. Cause the puppies are outside their sacks and awake so they can eat without the cord.

BOBBY. Gaaahhh . . .

MARLENE. Everything, well just about everything, has one.

JIMMIE. Really?

STACY. People?

BOBBY. Has Butch got one?

MARLENE. Yes.

CARLA. Who's Butch?

MARLENE. The baby. That's the name they decided on. Butch.

LORETTE. Thought it was a girl.

MARLENE. Don't make any difference to them. Still Butch. Right?

JIMMIE/BOBBY. Right.

JIMMIE. Has Butch got a cord too?

MARLENE. Yes. Right now she's probably curled up asleep, eating a meal.

JIMMIE. Really!

MARLENE. You had cords too. What do you think those are?

JIMMIE. Belly buttons.

MARLENE. That's where your cord was.

STACY. Me too?

MARLENE. Everybody.

JIMMIE. Did you have to chew it off?

MARLENE. No. The doctor cut it off and tied it up in a knot and stuffed it in and made you a belly button.

STACY. Oh, gross!

MARLENE. If he hadn't done that, we'd all be strung together like this. And we'd have to walk around like this. (*MARLENE holds the boys and waddles about. STACY joins them.*) We'd all be stuck together. Forever. Bumping into one another. (*The children all laugh.*) If I turned this way . . . then you'd have to turn. If I walked up stairs, you'd have to go up too . . .

(*MARLENE starts up the steps with the children, she stops short when she hears the whistle blow. The whistle's blast splits through the laughter and echoes over the country side. A dog howls. Silence for several seconds . . .*)

BOBBY. Momma?

JIMMIE. What's wrong?

MARLENE. Nothin'. Nothin' is wrong.

JIMMIE. You alright?

MARLENE. Of course I am.

STACY. (*to CARLA*) What was that?

MARLENE. But you know what? I think we woke up Butch. She's movin' around in there, kickin' up a storm. You wanna feel?

BOBBY. Yeah.

JIMMIE. Me too.

MARLENE. Here. Feel right there. Be careful. You feel that? (*The boys shake their heads "No".*) Right there. Can you feel it?

BOBBY. Gaahhh . . .

JIMMIE. I think I feel one of her toes!

MARLENE. Stacy, you wanna feel?

STACY. No.

MARLENE. You sure?

STACY. Uh huh.

MARLENE. Boys, let's give Butch a rest.

JIMMIE. You're sweating.

MARLENE. I know. It's hot and I'm a little tired. Why don't you run along and play. Let me rest.

JIMMIE. Alright.

BOBBY. Come on, Stacy.

JIMMIE. Let's check the trap. (*JIMMIE dashes off.*)

BOBBY. Beat you!

STACY. Wait for me . . . (*All three children race off-stage.*)

CARLA. What'd it mean?

MARLENE. Someone's hurt.

LORETTE. We don't know that.

CARLA. What should we do?

LORETTE. Nothin'.

CARLA. Maybe we should go over . . .

MARLENE. No!

LORETTE. We wait. That's what we do . . .

MARLENE. Everything'll be fine. Don't think about it. (*MARLENE picks up one of her magazines. CARLA and LORETTE half-heartedly start another card game. Several seconds of silence while LORETTE shuffles the cards.*)

CARLA. Was it hard bein' a secretary?

LORETTE. Huh?

CARLA. When you was a secretary, was it hard?

LORETTE. You type an awful lot, but you get to smoke and have coffee when you want. Your ass gets wide though from all the sittin'.

CARLA. I wouldn't like that. I always had a good butt.

LORETTE. Me too. I use to have dimples on both cheeks. Now they're on my thighs.

CARLA. That was the first thing Larry said he noticed

about me . . . was my butt. The way it moved when I carried the trays. Horniest devil that ever crawled into the back seat of a GTO. But we sure don't crawl into the back seat no more. Now its too much trouble for him to roll over to my side of the bed.

MARLENE. Big Jim's the same way. All men are like that. He hasn't touched me for months. But I understand. It's because he don't want nothin' to go wrong with the baby. You shouldn't take it personal. Men don't need it as much after they get married. Bean Jar Theory proves that.

CARLA. The what?

MARLENE. The Bean Jar Theory. If you took a big jar, and every time you had sex before you were married you put a bean *in*, and then after you're married, every time you had sex, you took a bean *out* . . . You'd never empty the jar. Fact. Swear to it.

CARLA. Well, I ain't took too many beans out lately.

MARLENE. Me neither.

CARLA. I ain't had a good bean in a long time.

LORETTE. Hell, I don't even remember what a bean looks like.

CARLA. You're not even married. You ain't got an excuse.

LORETTE. Charlie and me get it together a couple times a year. If it's a good year. (*They laugh.*)

CARLA. Larry and me use to make love all night long. Parked up on Walker's Hill. Tape deck playin', windows steamed up . . . Sometimes we wouldn't do anything but hold one another. Real tight. And wait for the sun to come up. (*CARLA's mood changes as she reflects.*) Then I got pregnant with Stacy . . . Our little bundle from Walker's Hill. (*beat*) He started changin' as soon as he found out I was pregnant. I look back now and I realize, he gave up. Stopped tryin' to please me. Stopped tryin' to get ahead. Just stopped. I think I saw the change comin', but I went ahead and married him anyway. I didn't know what else to do. Quit school and married Larry. Never graduated. Never got my diploma . . .

MARLENE. It's what you wanted.

CARLA. I thought it was. You know, when I started high school, I only wanted three things out of life. To be cheerleader. To graduate. And to get married. I got one of the three.

MARLENE. The most important one.

CARLA. I had such high hopes. Not for me, but for Larry. I just knew my husband was goin' to be somethin' special. He had looks. Everyone liked him. He talked about goin' to college on the GI Bill. He had so much goin' for him. Then he stopped tryin'. Bought his first dog right after Stacy was born. Then a second and a third. Now a whole kennel full. He just . . . went to the dogs. How's that for a joke?

LORETTE. Pretty weak.

CARLA. Sometimes, I look at Stacy and I think, "If only you hadn't come along . . .

MARLENE. Oh, Carla.

CARLA. Or if I'd never gone up to Walker's Hill or seen that damn GTO, I wouldn't be livin' like this. Wastin' my life . . .

MARLENE. It's the heat makin' you feel so restless.

CARLA. It's not the heat. I feel like this all the time. That there's got to be more. That I'm missin' out on somethin'.

MARLENE. You need a hobby.

CARLA. Marlene, I don't want a hobby . . .

MARLENE. You could macrame or crochet.

CARLA. I don't wanna . . .

MARLENE. Or sell Tupperware!

CARLA. I don't want to just fill my time. I want to do somethin'.

MARLENE. Well, I never wanted to be cheerleader or none of that stuff. I always had Big Jim.

CARLA. Ain't you ever had dreams for yourself? Don't you dream?

MARLENE. Oh, sure. I day dream all the time about bein' on Johnny Carson . . . What I'd wear and what I'd talk about. But everybody does that.

CARLA. I don't mean day dreamin'. I mean ambitions. To go and do.

MARLENE. Go and do what?

CARLA. Somethin'! Don't you ever feel like you were meant to do somethin'? I feel like I'm destined for somethin'. You know what destiny means? It means, "meant to do somethin' big." Somethin' big waitin' for you.

LORETTE. Carla, you know what you're sayin'?

CARLA. I know I could never be a country and western singer or a movie star like in those magazines. But I do have a lot to offer.

MARLENE. We know that.

CARLA. I ain't no starlet, but I can be pretty if I have a little make-up and get my hair fixed up. I can talk to people real good. I ain't bashful. And I'm smart. I ain't got a high school diploma, but I got a lot of common sense. And that's very important. Take you a long way. You see, Marlene, I know I could be good at somethin' if I just knew what it was. If I could just find it.

MARLENE. You'll find it.

CARLA. Not here I won't! There ain't nothin' here.

You want to know why me and Larry ain't had another baby? I don't want one. I don't want to raise another baby if this is all they'll ever get out of life. All they'll ever know . . . (*MARLENE stops, closes her magazine. CARLA realizes what she has done.*) I'm sorry. I didn't mean it.

MARLENE. I know you didn't.

CARLA. It just came out.

LORETTE. I think we all need to settle down.

CARLA. I'm sorry.

LORETTE. Maybe go home and get away from one another for a while.

MARLENE. Carla, what is it? What's really botherin' you?

CARLA. I told you I'm sick of waitin'.

MARLENE. No. It's not that.

CARLA. We have been sittin' here doin' nothin' for over two hours. We should of gone over there.

MARLENE. You don't want to go over there or you would have by now. It's Wanda ain't it? You're still thinkin' about her and Larry.

CARLA. I don't want to talk about it.

MARLENE. You haven't said a word . . .

CARLA. I don't want to talk about it, Marlene.

MARLENE. You always say you *don't* want to talk about somethin' when you *do* want to talk about somethin'.

CARLA. Well, I don't.

MARLENE. Don't let it bother you, Larry's seein' Wanda. It don't mean Larry doesn't love you. He does. Now, listen to me. Some men, not all of them, but some, have to mess around once in a while in order to feel . . . more like a man. It's not that they don't love you. They do. It's just they get bored or want to feel more man-like. And that's one way of doin' it. Sort of like racin' trucks or huntin'.

CARLA. What the hell are you talkin' about? Racin' trucks!

MARLENE. You don't understand do you?

CARLA. About racin' trucks?

MARLENE. I'm just tryin' to tell you how it is.

CARLA. How is it, Marlene? You tell me.

MARLENE. What I'm tryin' to say is that men are different than women.

CARLA. No shit.

MARLENE. They can mess around and it don't mean nothin'. A man can still love you, even if he's seein' another woman. Right, Lorette?

LORETTE. Don't involve me . . .

CARLA. You dumb shit!

MARLENE. What!

CARLA. If you only knew . . .

LORETTE. I've had enough!

MARLENE. What does that mean?

LORETTE. I don't want to listen to you two argue. (*Sirens are faintly audible. None of the women notice.*)

CARLA. Who are you? Miss Perfect!

LORETTE. No, smart ass. But I don't feel like sittin' out here and listening to you pick one another apart.

MARLENE. We ain't pickin' . . .

LORETTE. I'm goin' home.

CARLA. Well, go.

LORETTE. (*gathering up the brochures*) I am.

CARLA. Take your cards and brochures . . .

(*The women hear the sirens, stop and listen. A dog cries one long howl as the sirens grow louder. The three women remain tense, unmoving. Finally, the sirens fade in the distance, and the women relax their positions. There is a long, awkward pause before anyone speaks.*)

LORETTE. I don't feel too good. Must be the heat. I think I want to lie down for a while.

CARLA. Sure . . .

MARLENE. Use my trailer. It's closer.

LORETTE. Alright.

MARLENE. I'll keep the kids out.

CARLA. You need anything? (*LORETTE shakes her head, "No".*) We'll let you know as soon as we find out somethin'.

LORETTE. Give a knock.

MARLENE. Lay down on the couch. It's more comfortable than the bed. Just push the toys and junk on the floor.

LORETTE. Thanks. Be sure and get me up as soon . . .

CARLA. We will. (*LORETTE gives a short laugh and tosses the brochures she's holding on the table.*)

LORETTE. An Ocean Paradise . . . (*LORETTE crosses to MARLENE'S trailer but stops and turns around.*) You know, this is the first time in nineteen years I kind of regret we never got married. Of course, it wouldn't change anything, but it might be nice. (*LORETTE goes inside the trailer. CARLA and MARLENE are quiet for several moments, then MARLENE picks up a magazine and begins to read. Long pause . . .*)

MARLENE. You think the ghost of Elvis really talked to this woman? She swears Elvis sends her messages through her poodle. (*beat*) That Jeff Bridges is cute, ain't he? I think he's better lookin' than his brother.

Don't you think? He was suppose to be seein' Farrah for a while. Lee didn't know it. Now she's seein' Ryan O'Neal. I kinda feel sorry for Lee. (*Sirens are heard again. MARLENE stops reading for a moment, then, with some effort, continues.*) You know who I really feel sorry for? Dinah Shore. She's had a rough time. Burt left her for that flyin' nun. That Sally Fields. He still loves Dinah, but he's seein' Sally cause she's younger. Sally. You like that name? Sally.

CARLA. Would you lay off that name crap? I'm sick of hearin' it.

MARLENE. I thought you wanted to help me pick out a name.

CARLA. Well, I don't. And I'm tired of those stupid stories.

MARLENE. They're not stupid.

CARLA. Yes, they are.

MARLENE. No, they're not.

CARLA. I don't want to hurt your feelin's, but those magazines are junk, Marlene. Trash junk!

MARLENE. Are not! Lots of people read them.

CARLA. Ignorant people.

MARLENE. That's not true.

CARLA. Only stupid people read that kind of stuff.

MARLENE. Are you sayin' I'm stupid?

CARLA. No.

MARLENE. Yes, you are.

CARLA. No, I'm not. I'm just sayin' you read junky magazines.

MARLENE. You're sayin' I'm stupid.

CARLA. Ok, Marlene. You're stupid! Stupid for readin' that junk. My god, you got a high school diploma. You graduated, I didn't.

MARLENE. So what!

CARLA. You're wastin' your time readin' that garbage. Worryin' about flyin' nuns and plucked eye brows. If I'd of graduated, I'd of done things by now. Been gone and got a job . . .

MARLENE. Excuses! That's all you got are excuses. You always got an excuse when you don't want to do somethin'. If you were really goin' to leave, you would of done it a long time ago.

CARLA. I will.

MARLENE. You don't really want to leave here. You always got an excuse to stay, or you wait for me to give you one so you don't have to go. You'll never leave here. Never!

CARLA. I swear I will.

MARLENE. Then go. Don't wait around. Go. But you ain't goin' to find nothin' better than what you got right here.

CARLA. I got nothin'.

MARLENE. You're like a little kid. Always wantin' somethin' you ain't got, lookin' for somethin' . . .

CARLA. I am meant for more than this.

MARLENE. More than what? There can't be more than your family. That's the most important thing in the world.

CARLA. Crap! That is a bunch of crap.

MARLENE. It is not. Stacy and Larry love you and need you.

CARLA. No they don't. Stacy ain't needed me since she learned how to walk. And Larry sure as hell don't.

MARLENE. You don't want to face the fact you love Larry, do you? Because you're afraid if you do, it'll keep you from leavin' and findin' your destiny or whatever it is you're lookin' for. But I got news for you, you don't find happiness. You create it.

CARLA. Who the hell are you to tell me what to do?

MARLENE. I thought I was your friend.

CARLA. You're nothin' but an ol' breed dog for Big Jim.

MARLENE. Don't talk about Big Jim.

CARLA. You're not any better than Margaret in there.

MARLENE. I ain't goin' to listen to you.

CARLA. That's why you can stomach this place.

MARLENE. (*picking up the magazines*) I'm goin' inside with Lorette . . .

CARLA. You sit around all day readin' those magazines, waitin' for Big fuckin' Jim to come home.

MARLENE. He is my husband. I love him!

CARLA. No! You worship him.

MARLENE. Just cause you're unhappy, don't start in on . . .

CARLA. Marlene.

MARLENE. We got somethin' special no one can take away.

CARLA. Open your eyes!

MARLENE. We need each other. And that's special.

CARLA. (*overlapping lines*) You're blind.

MARLENE. He's special.

CARLA. You don't have any idea.

MARLENE. I am his wife . . .

CARLA. You don't know . . .

MARLENE. . . . and he is my husband!

CARLA. . . . about him and Wanda! (*pause*)

MARLENE. (*harsh whisper*) That is a lie.

CARLA. I didn't mean . . . It just came out.

MARLENE. It is a lie.

CARLA. I'm sorry, Marlene. But it is not a lie.

MARLENE. It is a lie.

CARLA. You ever wonder why he don't touch you no more? Why he ain't layed a hand on you in months?

MARLENE. I'm pregnant.

CARLA. That's an excuse.

MARLENE. He don't want nothin' to go wrong.

CARLA. An excuse. Cause he's seein' Wanda.

MARLENE. Lie.

CARLA. For months.

MARLENE. Liar.

CARLA. Marlene . . .

MARLENE. Lie!

CARLA. They're sleepin' together!

MARLENE. (*breaks down*) Lie! Lie! Lie! Lie . . . . . . (*It is quiet for several moments. CARLA moves to MARLENE.*)

CARLA. It's the truth, Marlene. Why do you think I hate her so much? Especially when you're so nice to her. I wanted to tell you, but I didn't want you to be hurt. I didn't want it to come out like this. You were so happy . . . (*pause*) But you got to face the facts. He's a man. Just like Larry. Like Cyril. He's not some sort of God. You got to realize that. Even though I wanted you to know, I hoped you'd never find out. But you had to sooner or later. They been together for months, ever since her husband died.

MARLENE. Before that.

CARLA. What?

MARLENE. Jim was seein' her before her husband died.

CARLA. You knew? (*MARLENE nods, "Yes."*) You knew about them?

MARLENE. From the start.

CARLA. All this time you knew.

MARLENE. Yes, Carla. I knew.

CARLA. Why? Why did you act like you didn't know?

MARLENE. Because I don't want to lose what I got. My husband. My children. My family. That's all I got. All I ever wanted. My whole life. I'd rather go on pretendin' and not think about it, than lose the only thing I've got.

CARLA. I didn't know.

MARLENE. Don't touch me!

CARLA. Oh, Marlene. I'm sorry.

MARLENE. Please stay away! Let me alone.

CARLA. I never worried about you, cause I didn't think you had any problems. That nothin' bothered you . . . Why didn't you tell me?

MARLENE. I want to go inside.

CARLA. Marlene, I love you. (*beat*) I never said that to you ever, I know. But I do. You know that don't you?

MARLENE. It's gettin' late. I need to start supper.

CARLA. I understand now. I do.

MARLENE. Just let me alone. (*MARLENE picks up the magazines and starts inside. An approaching truck is heard. Both women stop.*)

CARLA. (*looking off*) It's Cyril . . . He's back. (*CARLA runs to MARLENE'S trailer and knocks on the door.*) Lorette? Get up. Cyril's back.

(*CYRIL enters. He is dirty, his shirt is torn and he is obviously exhausted. He hesitates before speaking.*)

CYRIL. You got any lemonade left?

MARLENE. It's inside.

CYRIL. Never mind. (*CYRIL crosses and drinks from the faucet as LORETTE comes out of the trailer.*)

LORETTE. We heard sirens.

CARLA. Who was it?

CYRIL. That was Larry. He's on his way to the hospital. They're takin' him to Welburn.

CARLA. The hospital?

CYRIL. Yes. Charlie's gone with him.

LORETTE. Is Charlie . . .

CYRIL. No. He's fine. Not even a scratch. He's ridin' along with Larry in the ambulance.

MARLENE. What about Big Jim? (*beat*) Cyril? What about Jim?

CYRIL. He . . . ah . . . I'm sorry, Marlene. (*MARLENE stares at CYRIL for several seconds without moving. Then . . .*)

MARLENE. I've got to clean up this mess. Get it cleaned up. Get supper for the boys and . . . Oh, my God!

CARLA. Marlene . . .

MARLENE. Stay away!

CARLA. Let me help you.

MARLENE. Stay away from me, please. I'm alright. I can manage alone. I've got to get supper for the boys and ah . . . (*to CYRIL*) Hand me that magazine, would you please? I'll take this stuff in the house and fix supper for . . . for . . . (*MARLENE begins to break, but gains control of herself. Then without looking up . . .*) Did he suffer?

CYRIL. No. He didn't suffer.

MARLENE. If you see the boys, send them in to me.

CYRIL. We will. (*MARLENE exits into her trailer. CARLA starts after her, but LORETTE stops her.*)

LORETTE. Let her alone.

CARLA. She needs me.

LORETTE. She needs to be alone.

CARLA. I got to help her.

CYRIL. She can handle it.

CARLA. You sure?

CYRIL. Yes.

LORETTE. Charlie's ok?

CYRIL. He was no where near the accident.

LORETTE. And Larry . . .

CARLA. How bad is he? He ain't goin' to die is he?

CYRIL. He's banged up pretty bad . . .

CARLA. He can't die!

CYRIL. He ain't gonna die.

CARLA. He can't.

CYRIL. He's not. His leg is broke and I think he's got some busted ribs, but he's goin' to live.

LORETTE. What was it?

CYRIL. (*lighting a cigarette*) It was dynamite. But they don't know why it went off like it did. It was big, ripped right through. There was a chain reaction. Blew most of the high wall away. Larry's end didn't get it that bad. But the other end, where Big Jim was . . . (*CYRIL takes a drag off the cigarette.*) Any way, Larry's goin' to be alright. In a lot of pain, but he's ok. He was up on the washer, got his leg caught in the rungs of the ladder. We had to rig up a sling to get him down to the ambulance. But he's tough as nails. And very lucky . . . Carla?

CARLA. I got to see him. I should be with him.

CYRIL. We'll go to the hospital . . .

CARLA. I'll go right now and . . . He's goin' to be ok?

CYRIL. He's goin' to live.

CARLA. You can take me, can't you? You say he's at Welburn?

CYRIL. Yeah.

CARLA. Lord, I look a mess to go to the hospital. Is my hair ok?

LORETTE. Yes.

CARLA. I better fix myself up a little. I'll change my blouse, run a brush through my hair, then I'll be ready to go. Only take a minute. (*CARLA rummages through the suitcases for a hair brush and a fresh blouse.*)

CYRIL. You'll need insurance papers.

CARLA. What?

CYRIL. Papers for insurance.

CARLA. I need them?

LORETTE. Your Blue Cross.

CARLA. Blue Cross. Yeah, I'll ah . . . I'm not sure where he keeps 'em.

LORETTE. I'll help you look.

CARLA. I think they're under the bed. I'll find them.

LORETTE. I'll give you a hand. (*LORETTE and CARLA go inside the trailer. CYRIL puts out his cigarette. He is on the verge of tears. The children are heard running up from the creek. CYRIL composes himself before they enter.*)

BOBBY. (*offstage*) Beat you, Jimmie!

STACY. Wait for me!

(*JIMMIE, BOBBY and STACY enter.*)

JIMMIE. Bobby, you're it.

BOBBY. No. Stacy's it.

STACY. Uh huh! I tagged Bobby.

BOBBY. I'm not it. I promise . . .

JIMMIE. Hey, Cyril. We heard a truck. Thought you was Dad. (*BOBBY sneaks up and tags JIMMIE.*)

BOBBY. Got cha! I was it. (*JIMMIE chases BOBBY.*)

JIMMIE. Hey . . .

CYRIL. Jimmie! Bobby! Come here.

BOBBY. What?

CYRIL. Quit runnin' around. Stacy, you come over here too.

STACY. Why?

CYRIL. I want you to go inside.

STACY. Why?

CYRIL. Go inside the trailer to your mother. Boys, come here.

STACY. What for?

CYRIL. You fellas are a mess. All dirty.

JIMMIE. So are you.

BOBBY. Yeah, so are you.

CYRIL. Come over here to the faucet and I'll clean you guys up. Stacy, please go inside.

STACY. Can Jimmie and Bobby come in?

CYRIL. No.

STACY. Can't we play with the puppies?

CYRIL. They have to go home. And you have to go inside. So go. Please.

STACY. Ahhhh . . . (*STACY exits into the trailer.*)

CYRIL. Bobby, let me see you . . . How'd you get so muddy?

BOBBY. We been throwin' mud pies.

CYRIL. Looks like you been catchin' 'em with your face.

JIMMIE. He eats 'em.

CYRIL. You eat mud pies?

BOBBY. Yep. They're good.

CYRIL. Turn your face this way . . .

JIMMIE. You want to see our trap?

CYRIL. I'll see it later.

BOBBY. It's really neat.

JIMMIE. Bobby ate the bait.

CYRIL. Listen fellas, I . . .

BOBBY. Why are you so dirty?

(*WANDA runs on from between the trailers. She stops when she sees the two boys with CYRIL.*)

JIMMIE. Hey, Wanda!

BOBBY. Hi.

WANDA. Hi, boys. (*to CYRIL*) I just heard.

CYRIL. (*leading the boys away*) Both of you guys listen to me . . .

BOBBY. (*to WANDA*) We made a trap.

JIMMIE. You want to see it?

CYRIL. Your mother asked me to . . .

JIMMIE. We put leaves over it.

CYRIL. Hey! I'm tryin' to tell you somethin'!

BOBBY. You can't see the rope . . .

CYRIL. Would you listen to me!

JIMMIE. We just want to show . . .

CYRIL. I asked you to listen to me! I want you to go inside to your mother.

BOBBY. What for?

CYRIL. You see . . . your daddy . . . Well, your mother needs to talk to you.

BOBBY. Why?

CYRIL. (*grabbing BOBBY*) Bobby, you're gonna have to be good and . . . Whatever she says to you, you listen to her real good. Both of you. You're her little men. And you have to listen and understand. Try and understand . . . You understand?

BOBBY. You're hurting my arm. (*CYRIL releases BOBBY. Beat.*)

CYRIL. Go on inside to your mother. (*JIMMIE and BOBBY look at CYRIL for a moment, then quietly start for the trailer.*)

CYRIL. Jimmie?

JIMMIE. Yeah.

CYRIL. If you boys want, I'll help you look for the pony later on. (*JIMMIE nods, then the two boys exit inside the trailer. CYRIL turns away and angrily kicks at something on the ground.*)

CYRIL. Damnit! Damn . . . (*CYRIL crosses and sits without speaking. WANDA moves to him.*)

WANDA. I came over as soon as I . . . ah . . . How's Marlene? (*CYRIL shrugs.*) Carla at the hospital?

CYRIL. Not yet. I'm gettin' ready to take her.

WANDA. Was there anybody else?

CYRIL. No, don't think so. But they're still diggin' out. (*beat*)

WANDA. Did you see him? (*Long pause. Finally, with some effort, CYRIL answers.*)

CYRIL. Yeah. I saw him. I saw . . .

WANDA. It's alright. It's alright.

(*CARLA bursts out of the trailer carrying a box filled with papers followed by LORETTE.*)

CARLA. I couldn't find the papers. I didn't know which ones they were . . . (*She sees WANDA.*) . . . so I brought the whole box. (*CARLA tosses the box on the table for CYRIL.*) They're in there somewhere. (*to LORETTE*) Is my hair ok?

LORETTE. It's fine.

CARLA. (*to CYRIL*) Only thing I found was his truck registration. But I didn't look too good.

CYRIL. I'll look.

CARLA. Is this blouse ok?

LORETTE. Why don't you slow down?

CARLA. We got to get there.

LORETTE. Well, slow down.

CARLA. Find the papers and we'll go.

CYRIL. He's got everything in here. Huntin' license . . .

(*STACY comes out of the trailer.*)

STACY. Momma?
CYRIL. . . . dog papers . . .
CARLA. What?
STACY. I want to go with you.
CARLA. You can't.
STACY. Why not?
LORETTE. They don't allow kids in the hospital rooms.
CARLA. That's right.
STACY. I want to see Daddy.
LORETTE. Stay here with me.
STACY. I want to go.
CARLA. No.
LORETTE. We'll watch TV.
STACY. I want to . . .
CARLA. You'll be in the way.
STACY. No I won't.
CARLA. Now hush up! (*CARLA smacks STACY on the bottom.*) You're stayin' here! (*STACY, in tears, runs behind the trailer.*)
LORETTE. You shouldn't of hit her.
CARLA. I didn't hurt her.
LORETTE. You still shouldn't of done it. (*LORETTE exits looking for STACY.*)
WANDA. She could stay with me. (*CARLA stops.*) I could watch her if Lorette wants to go . . .
CARLA. Don't worry about it. It's none of your damn business.
CYRIL. She's only tryin' to help.

CARLA. I don't need her help.

WANDA. Carla, wait a minute . . .

CARLA. You got your nerve, comin' around here.

WANDA. Now, wait.

CARLA. Especially now.

WANDA. Would you listen! (*beat*) I know you hate my guts. And it doesn't make a bit of difference to me, so you can think what you want. But you should know, I lied today . . . about Larry's scar. I did it on purpose, cause I knew how you'd react. I did it for spite and I'm not sorry. I'm not apologizing.

LORETTE. (*offstage*) Stacy? Honey, where are you? Don't hide from me.

WANDA. I just want you to know, there was nothin' between me and Larry. Only reason I knew about that scar is I heard him and some guys braggin' one night at the bowling alley about how many scars they had. That's how I knew. Honest. We never . . . There was nothin' between us, ever. (*The two women look at one another for several moments. Then . . .*)

CARLA. I wish you had a story like that for Marlene. Cyril, find those papers and let's get out of here.

(*LORETTE enters with STACY.*)

LORETTE. Come on, now. She didn't hurt you. Don't cry.

STACY. I'm not.

LORETTE. Here we are. I found her.

CARLA. Stacy, I'm sorry I hit you, but I'm in a hurry. (*WANDA turns to CYRIL as she starts to exit.*)

WANDA. If I can help, or anybody needs anything . . .

CYRIL. I'll let you know.

CARLA. (*to STACY*) Don't be mad. Look at me.

CYRIL. (*to WANDA*) Thanks.

WANDA. Yeah. (*WANDA exits.*)

LORETTE. (*to STACY*) Go wash your face.

CARLA. I'll tell Daddy you're worried about him.

STACY. I don't care.

CARLA. He needs me. I gotta help him. And you're gonna have to help too. When I get back, we're gonna fix it up special for Daddy. You're gonna be his nurse. You want to be a nurse?

STACY. I don't care. (*STACY runs inside the trailer.*)

CARLA. If I'm not back in time, will you see she gets supper?

LORETTE. Of course.

CARLA. She'll eat anything, 'cept squash. I should be back by then, but if they keep Larry, I might have to stay.

LORETTE. You go on and do what you have to do.

CARLA. Where's my hair brush?

LORETTE. How's it comin', Cyril?

CARLA. She can stay up as late as she wants, but don't let her handle the puppies too much. (*CARLA has dug the hair brush out of the suitcase and crossed to the trailer's porch.*)

CYRIL. (*to LORETTE*) Those puppies. I tell you, that's the first thing Larry said to me.

CARLA. (*studying the steps*) I hope he can make it into the trailer.

CYRIL. We was carryin' him to the ambulance, and he opens one eye, I didn't even think he was conscious. But he looks up at me and says, "Take care of Margaret and the puppies for me. Make sure they get water." (*CARLA stops. CYRIL doesn't notice and continues talking.*) I tell you, he's a tough one. Layin' there all banged up. Didn't say a word about the pain or nothin'.

Only those puppies . . . (*CARLA drops the hair brush. She crosses to the faucet and fills a bucket with water as LORETTE finds the insurance papers.*)

LORETTE. Is this it?

CYRIL. Yeah, here we are. This is what we need. You ready?

LORETTE. Carla?

CYRIL. Let's go.

LORETTE. What is it?

CYRIL. What are you doin? (*CARLA grabs the mop and crosses to the trailer door, props it open and begins mopping.*) This is not the time for that.

CARLA. If Larry wants 'em to have water, they'll get water. Larry wants 'em fed . . .

CYRIL. You don't have to do that now.

CARLA. If Larry wants me to clean up, by God, I'll clean up.

LORETTE. I'll do that for you. You go to the hos . . .

CARLA. I'm gonna do it!

CYRIL. Hey! You're takin' it all wrong. He didn't know what he was sayin'. He was out of his head, in shock. He didn't know.

CARLA. Didn't know! My God, Cyril! I have been runnin' around like a fool, out of my head with worry, and he asks about a dog. A dog!

CYRIL. Settle down.

CARLA. Shut up and get out of my way.

CYRIL. Don't start in on me!

STACY. (*inside the trailer*) Momma!

LORETTE. Carla! You're gettin' blood everywhere.

CYRIL. Put that mop down.

LORETTE. I said I'd do it.

STACY. (*from inside.*) Momma, stop it.

CARLA. Get back in the trailer.

CYRIL. Give me the mop.

CARLA. Let go . . .

CYRIL. Give me that mop!

CARLA. No!

CYRIL. Carla . . .

CARLA. Damn you! Let go! (*CYRIL jerks the mop away from CARLA.*)

CYRIL. Now you settle down! Do you hear me? Settle down or I'll . . . (*CYRIL throws the mop.*) Just stop!

CARLA. I don't have to do anything . . . (*CYRIL grabs CARLA and pins her against the trailer.*)

CYRIL. Damnit, Carla! You're not the only person in the world.

CARLA. Don't you think I know that!

CYRIL. Marlene is in there with those boys tryin' to tell them they ain't got a daddy. And you. Damn you! You're actin' like . . . Your husband is alive. He wasn't in the truck with Jim. Sealed in the cab. Buried. Gas leakin'. I saw their daddy. By the time we dug him out, he was blue and swollen. His finger nails were ripped off . . .

CARLA. No.

CYRIL. . . . from clawin' for air.

CARLA. Please.

CYRIL. Clawin' while he died!

CARLA. Don't!

CYRIL. If Marlene can face those boys, you can at least . . .

CARLA. (*crying out*) I AM NOT MARLENE! I can't be what she is. I can't! (*CARLA, in tears, breaks free from CYRIL.*) Marlene knew! All this time she knew. I thought she was the one person, in the whole world, who was happy. Inside. I thought if I got away, I'd find the same thing. I'd stop wantin' . . . (*CARLA slides down the side of the trailer and sits on the porch.*)

CYRIL. Carla . . .

CARLA. Ever since I was a little girl, I dreamed . . . felt . . . there had to be more than what I had. Somethin' was missin'. I thought when I married Larry, I'd find it. Or when I had Stacy and became a mother it would happen. But it didn't. I blamed them . . . I thought I'd find it, somewhere. But I won't find it, will I Lorette? It's me. There's nothin' to find. It's me, right? (*CYRIL walks away. LORETTE crosses to CARLA as STACY watches from inside the trailer.*)

LORETTE. (*holding a tissue*) Here. Blow your nose. (*CARLA does.*) If you go to the hospital, you go because you want to, because you want to stay and make things work out, not because you feel sorry for him. If you can't do that . . . (*LORETTE pulls money out of the envelope and offers it to CARLA.*) Take this and leave.

CARLA. That's your retirement money.

LORETTE. I know what it is.

CARLA. But you and Charlie?

LORETTE. Me and Charlie can get along fine. I don't need Florida anyway.

CARLA. (*pulling away*) I couldn't take it.

LORETTE. Accept it as a loan. Go ahead, take it. (*LORETTE places the money in CARLA'S hand. She stares at CARLA for a moment, then crosses to CYRIL. STACY comes out of the trailer.*)

STACY. Momma?

CARLA. Come here. (*CARLA takes STACY and cradles her in her arms.*)

LORETTE. (*to CYRIL*) You goin' to the hospital?

CYRIL. Figured I would.

LORETTE. On your way, take her wherever she wants to go.

CYRIL. Alright.

STACY. Mom?

CARLA. What?

STACY. Are you still mad at me?

CARLA. No.

STACY. Are you gonna leave?

CYRIL. (*picking up a suitcase*) I'm on my way to Welburn. I'll take you wherever you want. Just tell me where. Gather up the rest of your things. (*CARLA looks at CYRIL holding the suitcase, then at STACY. Pause. CARLA wipes her eyes and stands up.*)

CARLA. You got those insurance papers?

CYRIL. Yes.

CARLA. I can take them. (*CYRIL hands her the papers.*) This all I need?

CYRIL. yes.

CARLA. Stacy, put your shoes on. We're goin' to the hospital.

STACY. Alright.

CARLA. You can put that down, Cyril. I won't be needin' it.

CYRIL. I'll start the truck. (*CYRIL puts the suitcase down and starts to exit. CARLA reaches out and touches his arm. They look at one another a moment, CYRIL smiles, then exits.*)

CARLA. Run a brush through your hair.

STACY. I will. (*CARLA crosses to LORETTE.*)

CARLA. Lorette . . . (*CARLA hands LORETTE the money. They both hold the money for a moment.*)

Thank you. (*beat*) It's me, right? (*LORETTE stares at CARLA without answering.*) Anything you want me to tell Charlie?

LORETTE. Yeah . . . Tell him to clip his toe nails. (*CARLA laughs.*) Just tell him to come home. That's all. (*LORETTE exits. CARLA turns and looks at MARLENE'S trailer for a moment, then to STACY.*)

CARLA. Come on, honey. Let's go. (*CARLA holds out her hand. STACY takes it and they both exit as the lights fade to black.*)

THE END

PROPERTY LIST

ON STAGE
Down Stage Right:
  Large tractor tire (filled with sand) DS.R
  Metal toy truck DS.R of sandbox
  Metal toy crane DS.L. of sandbox
  Stuffed doll (Holly Hobbie) sitting U.R. on tire
  Stuffed animal (moose) sitting U.L. on tire
  Plastic cup and saucer in sand
Stage Right Trailer (Marlene's):
  Cement block steps under door
  Metal toy dump truck DS.R. of steps
  Charcoal grill US.R. of steps against trailer
  Open bag of charcoal at base of grill
  Plastic cooler, various toys, and household items seen
    under trailer
Stage Left Trailer (Carla's):
  Metal pail with mop US.R. of porch against trailer
  Large metal tub under water faucet
  Plastic chaise lounge folded up against trailer DS. of
    faucet
Center Stage:
  Green metal patio table
  Green metal patio chair with arms S.R. of facing DS.L.
  Armless kitchen chair US. of table, facing table,
    pushed in
  Armless kitchen chair S.L. of table, facing DS.
  Empty Spic-N-Span box on table

OFF STAGE
In Stage Right Trailer (Marlene's):
  3 or 4 movie magazines (inc. a National Enquirer)

Horse bridle
Plastic bag of carrots
Plastic pitcher of lemonade
Tray
3 plastic glasses
Under Stage Right Trailer:
  Length of rope (approx. 3′)
Up Stage Left:
  Lorette's sewing bag
    —Camel cigarettes
    —Lighter
    —Bean bag ash tray
    —Deck of cards
    —2 pairs of mens socks with holes in the toes
    —pincushion with needle
    —2 spools of thread (matching color of socks)
  Travel brochures
  Large envelope (with money)
  Coffee mug with coffee
  Stacy's white shoes
  Cyril's Pall Mall cigarettes and matches
In Stage Left Trailer (Carla's):
  Suitcase with stand-up back
    —unfolded clothes
    —red bikini underwear
  Travel case
    —stand-up mirror
    —brush and comb
    —hair clips
    —nail polish
  Shopping bag with handles with Stacy's clothes
  Button up plaid blouse (Carla)
  Shoebox with legal papers
    —insurance papers

Dog bowl
Small plastic basin

INTERMISSION SCENE CHANGES
Strike Spic-N-Span box
Set stuffed animal in sand
Strike pitcher, tray, and 3 glasses
Strike plastic cup and saucer
Strike nail polish
Set playing cards in a stack US. on table
Set travel case on flower box
Set brush, comb, and mirror in travel box
Set suitcase D.L. by faucet
Set magazines on table
Set red food coloring on floor inside door of S.L.
    trailer*

---

*This is used as blood in the last scene when Carla wet mops the
trailer.

COSTUME PLOT

STACY
dirty blue shorts
dirty white flowered T-shirt
white dusty sandals (see property list)
hair in a pony tail
skin tanned

CARLA
denim cut-off shorts
blue and white striped midriff shirt (ties in front)
brown thongs
thin gold wedding band
skin tanned
later wears the button up plaid blouse (see property list)

CYRIL
Act I:
dark green work T-shirt
tan work pants
black belt
black work boots
clean white bandage wrapped around left hand
skin tanned
Act II:
dark green work shirt smeared with mud and coal dirt
tan work pants smeared with mud and coal dirt
handkerchief in back pocket
bandage dirty
skin and hair dirty

MARLENE
  pregnant padding
  sleeveless maternity housedress
  thongs
  gold wedding band
  skin pink on the shoulders
JIMMIE
  dirty cut-off denim shorts
  dirty tank top
  skin tanned
  no shoes
BOBBY
  same as Jimmie
WANDA
  tight green pants
  white tube top
  green plaid blouse rolled up at the sleeves and tied at
    the waist
  tan high heels
  beehive hair style of the 1950's
  skin tanned
LORETTE
  short sleeved button up spring housecoat
  kleenex in the pocket
  glasses worn on a chain around her neck
  thongs
  hair worn in a hair net
  no tan

EFFECTS PLOT

Act I
1. Country western music X-fade to . . .
2. Station ID X-fade to . . .
3. Music from inside of the trailer
4. Distant explosion and dogs barking
5. Distant explosion and dogs barking
6. Distant explosion and dogs barking
7. Loud series of explosions and dogs howling
8. Country western music

Act II
9. Country western music
10. Town whistle
11. Sirens
12. Sirens
13. Truck pulling in and truck door slam
14. Country western music

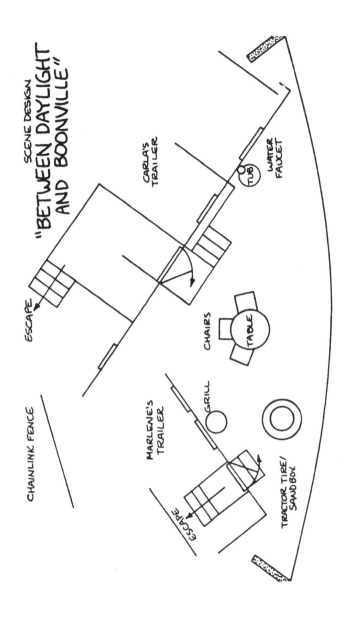

SCENE DESIGN
"BETWEEN DAYLIGHT AND BOONVILLE"

CARLA'S TRAILER

TUB

WATER FAUCET

ESCAPE

CHAINLINK FENCE

CHAIRS

TABLE

MARLENE'S TRAILER

GRILL

ESCAPE

TRACTOR TIRE/ SANDBOX

OTHER TITLES AVAILABLE FROM SAMUEL FRENCH

THREE YEARS FROM "THIRTY"
Mike O'Malley

Comic Drama / 4m, 3f / Unit set

This funny, poignant story of a group of 27-year-olds who have known each other since college sold out during its limited run at New York City's Sanford Meisner Theater. Jessica Titus, a frustrated actress living in Boston, has become distraught over local job opportunities and she is feeling trapped in her long standing relationship with her boyfriend Tom. She suddenly decides to pursue her dreams in New York City. Unbeknownst to her, Tom plans to propose on the evening she has chosen to leave him. The ensuing conflict ripples through their lives and the lives of their roommates and friends, leaving all of them to reconsider their careers, the paths of their souls and the questions, demands and definition of commitment.

OTHER TITLES AVAILABLE FROM SAMUEL FRENCH

THE CEMETERY CLUB
Ivan Menchell

Comedy / 1m, 5f / Multiple Sets

Three Jewish widows meet once a month for tea before going to visit their husband's graves. Ida is sweet tempered and ready to begin a new life, Lucille is a feisty embodiment of the girl who just wants to have fun, and Doris is priggish and judgmental, particularly when Sam the butcher enters the scene. He meets the widows while visiting his wife's grave. Doris and Lucille squash the budding romance between Sam and Ida. They are guilt stricken when this nearly breaks Ida's heart. The Broadway production starred Eileen Heckart as Lucille.

"Funny, sweet tempered, moving."
– *Boston Globe*

"Very touching and humorous. An evening of pure pleasure that will make you glad you went to the theatre."
– *Washington Journal Newspapers*

OTHER TITLES AVAILABLE FROM SAMUEL FRENCH

THE RIVERS AND RAVINES
Heather McDonald

Drama / 9m, 5f / Unit Set

Originally produced to acclaim by Washington D.C.'s famed Arena Stage. This is an engrossing political drama about the contemporary farm crisis in America and its effect on rural communities.

"A haunting and emotionally draining play. A community of farmers and ranchers in a small Colorado town disintegrates under the weight of failure and thwarted ambitions. Most of the farmers, their spouses, children, clergyman, banker and greasy spoon proprietress survive, but it is survival without triumph. This is an *Our Town* for the 80's."
– *The Washington Post*

DANGER- GIRLS WORKING
James Reach

Mystery Comedy / 11f / Unit Set

At a New York girl's boarding house, there is a newspaper woman who wants to write a novel, a wise cracking shop girl, the serious music student, a faded actress, a girl looking for romance, the kid who wants to crash Broadway and other boarders. The landlady, is the proud custodian of the "McCarthy Collection," a group of perfect uncut diamonds. When it disappears from the safe, the newspaper woman is given two hours to solve the case before the police are called. Suspicion is cleverly shifted from one to the other of the girls and there's a very surprising solution.